Crosscurrents / MODERN CRITIQUES

Harry T. Moore, *General Editor*

The Modern Italian Novel
FROM CAPUANA TO TOZZI

Sergio Pacifici

WITH A PREFACE BY

Harry T. Moore

SOUTHERN ILLINOIS UNIVERSITY PRESS
Carbondale and Edwardsville

FEFFER & SIMONS, INC.
London and Amsterdam

For Rigo,
Paul and Jackie,
Jimmy and Dodo,
Michael and Nancy,
sweet friends
with much love

Library of Congress Cataloging in Publication Data

Pacifici, Sergio.
  The modern Italian novel from Capuana to Tozzi.

  (Crosscurrents: modern critiques)
  Bibliography: p.
  1. Italian fiction—19th century—History and
criticism. 2. Italian fiction—20th century—History
and criticism. I. Title.
PQ4173.P28   853'.03   75–156786
ISBN 0–8093–0614-X

Contents

Contents

Preface

In 1967, Sergio Pacifici brought out *The Modern Italian Novel from Manzoni to Svevo* in the Crosscurrents/Modern Critiques series. At that time we considered it the first of two volumes, but as Professor Pacifici began to work with the later material, he found that a total of three would be needed to deal with his subject thoroughly. His first book has done well, in terms of critical approval and general sales, and we have agreed with him that his study really needs to be published in three units, keeping each of them at the length deemed necessary for individual Crosscurrents volumes. So here is *The Modern Italian Novel from Capuana to Tozzi*.

After Dr. Pacifici's opening chapter, "Background of the Italian Novel," we find essays appearing on such writers as Gabriele d'Annunzio, Giuseppe A. Borgese, and Luigi Pirandello. He also discusses the work of three women writers, including Grazia Deledda, who in 1926 won the Nobel Prize for literature. With these authors and several others he examines, we have another installment of the only recent study in English of the modern Italian novel. And we can look forward to the third volume, which of course will have Alberto Moravia and Ignazio Silone, among others.

Several of the authors in the present list will be unknown to many of us who have not followed twentieth-century Italian literature closely. This applies especially to the last writer whom Professor Pacifici treats: Federigo Tozzi. But,

vii

as the author points out, Tozzi's true value is only now being
recognized by his fellow countrymen.

Some of us will remember reading d'Annunzio in our teens,
particularly *Il piacere*, which we encountered in its English
translation as *The Child of Pleasure*. This is the d'Annunzio
novel Dr. Pacifici concentrates on. It appeared in Italy in
1889; the first New York edition came out in 1896. It was
fairly "old stuff" when some of us adolescents discovered it
many years later—but it had a punch.

Professor Pacifici rightly points out that d'Annunzio was,
in that story, dealing with a decadent Roman society in the
period after the Risorgimento. Of course—but those of us
over here who encountered it in our early youth didn't know
what decadence was; we merely surmised that most European
adults who were at least fairly well off behaved like the
characters in d'Annunzio's book. Count Andrea Spirelli, the
protagonist, had an ideal life, divided between poetry and
women, the latter taking up the greater amount of time.
We thought of him riding along the Corso in open carriages,
accompanied by a principessa or a visiting diplomat's wife,
women who wore long white gloves and sinned elegantly.
(My first copy of this book was taken from me by Authority,
so I at once bought another.)

The young people who read today's "porno" novels encounter something quite different and far more graphic—
a literature that already shows signs of wearing itself out
(consider the recent failure, in New York, of the Olympia
Press, which unsuccessfully imported itself from Paris).
Lawrence and Joyce won't fade because, behind their candor,
they are great artists.

However "shocking" d'Annunzio may have been when
some of us were young, the erotic parts of his work now appear to be tame. And d'Annunzio is largely forgotten in
English-speaking countries now. But those of us who knew
his work a few decades ago have retained at least one impression: brown-yellow modern Rome. The ruins of empire rise
jaggedly on every side, but they are overshadowed by all
the baroque domes and more recent buildings. Because of
early atmospheric innoculation by d'Annunzio, we have a

special feeling for modern Rome, a feeling not diminished even by today's automobile traffic.

Professor Pacifici doesn't discuss all of d'Annunzio's novels, though along with his rather full treatment of *The Child of Pleasure* he mentions certain others as comprising "most of his fiction." One of these in *Il fuoco* (1900), translated (in my now-out-of-print Modern Library copy) as *The Flame of Life*. This is the autobiographical novel about the author's love affair with Eleonora Duse. Early in the story the poet-hero Stelio Effrena addresses an aristocratic audience, including the Queen, in the Doge's Palace in Venice: his megalomaniac oratory discourages many readers from going on to later passages.

Yet, for all his faults, d'Annunzio was an important influence on his time. And Sergio Pacifici gives his work just the right emphasis. He also provides us with a highly interesting account of d'Annunzio's vivid life.

Another of these authors I'll mention is one whom some of us knew in a later phase of our lives than the one in which we absorbed d'Annunzio. This is G. A. Borgese who, as Dr. Pacifici notes, refused to take the oath which Mussolini required of all teachers in 1931; Borgese exiled himself and taught at a number of American universities. While in the United States he married Thomas Mann's daughter Elizabeth, who also became an author.

Professor Pacifici discusses Borgese in terms of the imaginative writers who were also critics, and he mentions a number of them, including Coleridge and Arnold. But within the scope of this book, its author couldn't spend much time on sidelights; he gives most of his discussion space to Borgese's outstanding novel, *Rubè* (1921), which he points out as a forerunner of Moravia's work. *Rubè* (published in the 1920s in an English translation by Isaac Goldberg, now out of print) is an important novel, a portrait of an intellectual trying to realize and maintain his identity in a confusing era. It is a significant twentieth-century novel which, we can hope, Professor Pacifici's comments might bring back into print.

To take up the matter of those sidelights which Dr.

Pacifici quite properly avoided, I want to mention Borgese's great historical volume, *Goliath: The March of Fascism*, which traced that movement back from Mussolini (whom Borgese knew personally) to roots in the Italian past; he showed the conflict between liberalism and authoritarianism in Italian history. But it was not only the brilliant investigations of Italy's past that made this book so remarkable—and it must be one of the finest books of history of our time— but also the author's mastery of English prose. This book deserves to be kept in print. (In Italy, the firm of Mondadori has re-issued Borgese's work in thirty volumes.)

Borgese, who died in Italy in 1952, shortly after his seventieth birthday, was a man of fire and energy. He looked like the portraits of Savanarola, but his ardor went in quite a different direction, a constructive one. It is good to read Professor Pacifici's examination of Borgese's finest novel, as it is good to read all his comments on these other authors.

With two fine volumes of his critical history of the modern Italian novel, we can look forward to the third. As noted earlier, these are the only studies of the Italian novel in English in a long while; specifically, since Domenico Vittorini's book of 1930 (reprinted in 1967, with no additions to the text). But Sergio Pacifici's work is more than unique; it is extremely valuable in itself.

HARRY T. MOORE

Southern Illinois University
September 21, 1972

Introduction

The present volume was originally supposed to be the second of a two-part study of the modern Italian novel. A realization that the abundance of the material would simply preclude the achievement of my objective led me to expand this project to three volumes. I am deeply indebted to Vernon Sternberg, Director of the Southern Illinois University Press, and Harry T. Moore, Editor of the Crosscurrents series, for supporting my decision.

The aims of this introductory study are simply to correct, modify, and otherwise extend present knowledge of the Italian novel in English-speaking countries; to try to answer, insofar as possible, certain basic questions students inevitably ask in connection with the novel in Italy: Who are the enduring novelists that country has produced over the past century or so? In what ways did they improve the native tradition of the genre? In what specific manner can we read such works as reflections of the vast social, political, and economic changes undergone by the nation? What insights into the human predicament do they offer to the reader of today, and how significant and relevant are such insights?

This book hardly claims to offer any final answers to these and other questions. It does propose, however, to prepare the initiate to begin grappling with them; and, by providing him with a certain amount of factual information and interpretative comments, it hopes to enable him to begin formulating independent, if tentative, judgments.

The scheme of this volume, like the one that preceded it and the one that will follow it, is simple. I have chosen a number of writers whose work seemed to be particularly apt to illustrate the development of the novel in modern Italy. Rather than attempting to study their entire literary production, I have generally limited myself to considering only the book or books that are most persuasively indicative of their vision as well as of the thematic, stylistic, and structural innovations they brought to the genre. Within the limitations of space, I have also touched briefly on those important biographical and literary events of my subjects when, by so doing, the meaning and significance of their work could be illuminated further. No detailed study of the selected number of writers included in this book has been attempted, and only two of them, for reasons which I trust my analyses will make clear, receive major treatment. The English translations of titles mentioned are given in brackets after the Italian titles. If the work has been published in an English translation the English title and publishing information appears in parentheses.

This book begins with Luigi Capuana and ends with Federigo Tozzi. With the exception of Marino Moretti, the writers discussed here are no longer living. The final volume of this history will overlap the second volume: it will begin with Aldo Palazzeschi and will end with the leading novelists of the 1950s.

I think it is only reasonable to point out that this history, the first to appear in English in more than forty years, is neither an exhaustive nor, much less, a definitive account of my subject. There are omissions of names and facts, and some of my informed readers may wish to challenge my selection, which has been at once critical and personal. Nevertheless, choices, difficult and troubling as they are, must be made. I offer no apologies for the writers left out other than to say that, even taking into account the nature of the present survey, I have rejected the alternative of presenting a catalogue *raisonné* of names and facts for a somewhat more detailed presentation of fewer novelists. Those readers wishing to extend their knowledge of the field, will find the bibliographical references particularly helpful. They include the most lucid and penetrating studies that have appeared in Italy (many of them quite recently) as well as some of the best material in English— material, I regret to say, often overlooked by Italian scholars.

My analyses are based upon a reading of the works in the original. In order to make the text easier to read, I have quoted from the standard English translations listed in each chapter. In all other cases, the translations are mine.

It is my sincere hope that this volume will begin filling a regrettable lacuna in Italian studies and that it will contribute to a firmer understanding of the novel. If it achieves its aim, the effort that went into writing it will prove to have been fully justified. I should feel doubly rewarded, however, if it will also stimulate others to restudy the relatively unexplored problem of the modern novel in Italy and offer other fresh interpretations of its quality and achievement.

I should like to acknowledge with deep gratitude the help and assistance of the staffs of the Yale University Sterling Memorial Library, the Paul Klapper Library of Queens College, and the Paterno Library of Columbia University, and in particular Messrs. Harry P. Harrison, Wendell Daniel, and John Connolly. I am also grateful to the Italian Cultural Institute of New York and its able Director, Professor Giuseppe Cardillo, for their numerous courtesies, and to the Cultural Division of the Italian Ministry for Foreign Affairs for a summer travel grant. I owe a very special debt to Mrs. Marjorie Waldman for the skill, competence, and cheerfulness with which she typed the various drafts and the final manuscript copy of this book. As always, I am grateful more than my words can express to my wife Jeanne and my daughters Tina and Sabrina for their constant encouragement and generous support.

SERGIO PACIFICI

Larchmont, New York
January 23, 1972

The Modern Italian Novel

FROM CAPUANA TO TOZZI

Background of the Modern Italian Novel

Eighteen sixty-one is a date that marks the most dramatic turning point in the history of modern Italy, opening a period of literary creativity that ranks with the best and most prolific in the culture of that country. "The unification of Italy," writes Massimo Salvadori in his study *Italy*, "was a political revolution. The real revolution—the transformation of a way of life resulting from changing ideas, values and attitudes—was slow in coming." From our own perspective, we can see that much that had taken place on the Italian literary scene from the early part of the century, and indeed in some cases even earlier, is a sort of prelude to the momentous changes that were to take place after the unification. A rather large number of poems and narratives written as early as the middle of the eighteenth century constitute stinging indictments of the arrogance, decadence, and inhumanity of the rulers oppressing the Italian peninsula. Giuseppe Parini's *Il giorno* (1763; *The Day*, London, 1927), Vittorio Alfieri's *Saul* (1782; *Saul*, London, 1815), Ugo Foscolo's *Le ultime lettere di Jacopo Ortis* (1802; *The Last Letters of Jacopo Ortis*, Chapel Hill, 1970), and Alessandro Manzoni's *I promessi sposi* (1842; *The Betrothed*, N.Y., 1956) are not just literary masterpieces. They are works of literature whose impact upon the cultivated audience was both vast and profound and, much like the novels of Dickens and Zola, must be evaluated with a different yardstick than the one normally used by literary critics. One of the major achievements of such and other works lies precisely in the large contribution they made to the shaping of a national consciousness and the development of a deep pride in an extraordinary cultural heritage no foreign tyrant could deny. Moreover, they instilled in the heart and soul of their readers a yearning to be free from all foreign rule, however benevolent or enlightened. The small nucleus of patriots and intellectuals who, in different ways and with different means, set out to promote the unification of their country understood clearly that unless complete freedom were achieved, their nation would continue to occupy a secondary place in the European political chessboard. The literary conspiracy in which many patriotic men engaged between 1830 and the middle of the century was effective in its two main aims: to discredit Austria (Italy's arch enemy) and to gradually bring about a feeling of revulsion against the abject condition of servitude the people of Italy had endured for far too many centuries. This activity soon spread to other fields, particularly music, and gained new and fresh impetus in the works of Rossini and Verdi whose operas *William Tell* and *The Lombards of the First Crusade* focused on the great themes of national pride and political unity. Literary and musical creativity and the sociopolitical plottings of underground groups (such as the *Carbonari*) became interacting dynamic forces that sprang from and further intensified a passionate resolve to achieve full freedom from all oppressors. The enormous success enjoyed by the spate of historical novels published between 1825 and 1850, even by such lesser works as Massimo D'Azeglio's *Ettore Fieramosca* (1833; Boston, 1859) and Tommaso Grossi's *Marco Visconti* (1834; N.Y., 1904), for example, was due to the fact that they addressed themselves to timely issues, now part and parcel of an ongoing political struggle.

The years following the unification proved to be substantially more awesome than most responsible political figures had dared to predict. Indeed, when placed in the new perspective, the wars of liberation seemed to have been a far easier task than the attainment of social, economic, and cultural unity so vital to any nation. The set of problems facing the state seemed to be almost unsurmountable: there was an impelling need to create a viable national administrative bureaucracy capable of earning the confidence of a people traditionally suspicious of central authority; the economy was sagging abysmally in the *Mezzogiorno* while relatively prospering in the north; illiteracy was incredibly high; discrimination against women, exploitation of the working class and the poor was a daily fact of life; the health of the populace was very poor and the corrective elements (doctors, medicines, and hospital) in short supply; the involvement of the people in the political process needed to be reassessed. All these and many additional problems demanded solutions and long-range planning that were particularly difficult to achieve because of the petty rivalry and deep-seated jealousy between and within political parties, a situation further aggravated by a general incapacity to put some of their ideological differences aside for the good of the nation. Only in 1882 did the restrictive voting laws begin to undergo a slow, measured process of liberalization, with the result that the number of enfranchised citizens rose to two million, or 7 percent of the total population. By and large, the government was more successful in its pursuit of modestly enlightened national policies than in its foreign policies, which proved to be divisive and disastrous, particularly in the ill-advised and ill-timed colonial adventures that resulted in humiliating defeats. Italy's alliance with her traditional enemy Austria also proved to be cause of much internal militancy. That the period under consideration was hectic and critical is mirrored in the thirty-eight different cabinets, whose average life was about two years, that governed the nation under three kings, none of whom was genuinely committed to a democratic parliamentary rule. Scandals of all sorts, political, military, and financial, rocked the nation, decreasing the people's confidence in their rulers. Violence was a clear manifestation of the general unhappiness of the citizenry with the manner in which their affairs were administered. In one year alone, 1901, there were about 1700 strikes during which 242 people lost their lives. In 1913 the number of strikes had appreciatively decreased while the participants had increased to 385,000.

While the state of the nation was frequently precarious and the road to real unification replete with numerous obstacles, some notable if not extraordinary progress was made in several areas. One that was to have a particular impact upon the cultural scene was the improvement of the education of the middle and working classes. The other was a substantially higher standard of living enjoyed by the peasantry and the working class. As in other European countries, the educational reforms instituted in the closing decades of the century produced an ever-larger reading public, a factor that was instrumental in giving birth to a more commercial type of literature. And this meant that at least a veritable cultural revolution was indeed at hand. In 1861, slightly more than 2.5 percent of the total population (or barely 630,000 people) could speak Italian in addition to their native dialect; of these, 66 percent lived in Tuscany, the cradle of the Italian tongue. An incredible percentage of the population, 78 percent nationally and 90 percent in the south, was illiterate. Forty years later, thanks to the enactment of several pieces of legislation (particularly the Coppino law prescribing free and compulsory education for children between the ages of six and nine), the percentage of illiterates had declined to 50 percent of the population. In 1870, slightly less than one and one-half million students filled 30,000 classrooms; in 1907, both the number of students and classrooms had doubled.

The benefits of political unification extended to other areas, such as freedom to travel and establish residence in other parts of the country. The mushrooming of newspapers and magazines of all political shades encouraged free expression and discouraged cultural parochialism. The general improvement of the educational system, the spread and acceptance of the national language, placed books and periodicals within the easy grasp of an ever-increasing public.

Writing shortly after the beginning of our century, the critic Renato Serra commented on the proliferation of publishing houses and periodicals which increased the opportunities for writers. In 1913, he noted, over 11,100 new titles had been published and were classified as follows: 300 collections of poetry; 415 novels; 651 philological works; 1601 histories and fine arts; 260 philosophical works, and some 750 periodicals. Linguistic unity, while by no means totally achieved, was moving closer to full realization. Again Renato Serra commented: "Everyone, in different manners, writes more or less the same language, with a certain amount of neatness, more than mere propriety and a choice and wealth of vocabulary such as we have seldom seen in Italy."

To assume that all these changes brought about a sustained improvement in national literary taste is, of course, unrealistic and questionable. Much as in other European countries, educational reforms, however sweeping, did not automatically produce a more sophisticated literature. As Walter Allen points out in his study *The English Novel,* "the gap between education and the worst was so great that the highbrow-lowbrow dichotomy with which we are so wearisomely familiar was inevitable." The books written with a certain audience in mind fared well, better than ever in fact: Guido da Verona, Carola Invernizio, and Luciano Zuccoli, all three lowbrow novelists, achieved huge success. Such was not the case of the more serious novelists: Verga's popularity decreased sharply after he stopped writing the sentimental, romantic novels of his first period; Italo Svevo achieved recognition (if only from the critics) shortly before his death in 1928; Luigi Pirandello, prolific and esteemed, found his public thanks to the controversy generated by his play *Sei personaggi in cerca d'autore* (1921; *Six Characters in Search of an Author,* N.Y., 1952); and Federigo Tozzi was to remain largely ignored until recent years. Another element of considerable import was the changing composition of the reading audience, now heavily made up of women. Because of practical and intellectual considerations the status of women was definitely enhanced: witness the growing number of women who soon became established writers and the emergence of a type of fiction (generally serialized in newspapers and magazines) with unmistakably feminine themes and outlook.

At least in one important way did the situation of the

novel change: while in the first three decades or so of the last century it would have been all but impossible to find a responsible critic who could bring himself to accept the worth and seriousness of the genre and recognize its quality on the same terms of poetry, more and more intellectuals now praised it and practised it widely. In an essay published in 1872, the authoritative critic Luigi Capuana (who would become a novelist shortly afterward) stressed the possibilities of the genre; the poet-novelist Antonio Fogazzaro called the novel "the prevailing expression of the poetic sentiment of our time"; Ugo Ojetti, after interviewing several intellectuals, reported that the novel was now considered "the best and the richest of possibilities." Finally, Gabriele d'Annunzio lavished praise on the genre, deeming it "destined to survive over any other [literary] form in the future," and most capable "to handle a vast aesthetic coordination of vital ingredients." Such hopeful views and optimistic forecasts, as we shall see, were to change materially at the end of the century.

Political unity and the changed social configuration it brought about meant also that a genre that had thrived during the *Risorgimento* years experienced a marked decline of interest. Thus, the historical novel, assiduously practised by writers who, according to Giorgio Petrocchi in his survey *Il romanzo storico italiano nell'800*, considered it "a proof of political apprenticeship for future political initiatives" lost much of its attraction. Not that it died altogether: on the contrary, for some time it continued to be practised by a number of fine novelists such as Ippolito Nievo, Giuseppe Rovani, and Federico De Roberto, all of whom sought to make the genre a vehicle capable of mirroring the nation's long struggle for political unification. Nievo died in 1861, without seeing in print his masterpiece, *Le confessioni di un italiano* (1863; *The Castle of Fratta*, Boston, 1958). Rovani, some thirteen years younger than Ippolito Nievo set himself to the task of composing a long novel, *Cento anni* [A hundred years] (1859–64), which offers even today a rather lively canvas of Italian and Milanese life between 1750 and 1850, written with the purpose of giving the reader a special feeling of what it was to have lived through that extraordinary period. Both Nievo and Rovani chose the cyclic approach for their novels, whose characters become actual participants of the historical process rather than its helpless victims, as had been the case in Manzoni's *The Betrothed*. Both novelists rejected the prevailing notion that the setting of the novel should be in the past, sufficiently remote to give the author a desirable perspective as well as a larger degree of freedom to isolate historical events and distort them if necessary to suit the demands of the plot. In this sense, they and others who soon followed in their paths showed a rather contemporary attitude of considering past history, as the late Marxist critic Georg Luckàcs would have it, "the pre-history of the present." Their works amounted to nothing less than an interpretation of an historical chapter in which they had been personally involved and had thus acquired a direct experience. Federico De Roberto's *I Vicerè* (1894; *The Viceroys*, N.Y., 1962), on the other hand, focused not on the problems of the *Risorgimento*, but on how its lofty ideals had mercilessly been betrayed by the ruling family of the Uzedas who managed to retain most of its power by clever political manipulation. History continued to haunt other novelists: Luigi Pirandello (who was to achieve his fame for his plays) made of the conflict between "the old and the young" the absorbing theme of a novel bearing the same title. But with De Roberto and Pirandello we sense that the historical novel concerned itself with not the glories of yesteryear and the hopes entertained by its heroes for a better, free Italy, but with what Carlo Salinari in his *Miti e coscienza del decadentismo italiano* calls "three collective failures: [the failure] of the *Risorgimento* as a general movement of renewal of our nation; of the Unification as an instrument of liberation and development of the most backward regions, and in particular of Sicily and the south; of socialism, which could have been the resumption of the *Risorgimento*, and had instead become lost in the sandbanks of the irresponsible lack of commitment of the leaders and the backwardness of the masses. . . . at the same time, we have [in the novel] the history of personal failures: of the older [generation], unable to move from ideals into reality, who found itself responsible for the scandals, the corruption, and bad government; of the young [generation] that felt stifled in an already crystallized society that did not allow action capable to change, and as such free expression of its personality."

De Roberto's *The Viceroys* and Pirandello's *The Old and the Young* appeared in 1894 and 1913 respectively. Yet, by the beginning of the 1880s the historical novel was already losing considerable ground to veristic fiction, in which the historical component had at best a marginal role.

Luigi Capuana and Giovanni Verga were the best exponents of the new school, the first at the theoretical, the second at the creative level. Among the radical innovations of *verismo* there was, first of all, a determination to deal with themes of extraordinary human relevance, evidenced by the manner in which it focused on the toils and sufferings of the peasants, the poor, the destitute, the exploited. The second feature of *verismo* was the use (and in some cases, the outright invention) of a direct, simple, unliterary style that resulted from a conviction that the novelist should steep himself in the oral tradition if he wished to create a live, believable language appropriate to his characters. To be sure, the problem of style was intimately connected with the broader *questione della lingua,* that is to say the necessity (particularly during the *Risorgimento* period) of writing in a language that could be nationally understood. Responding to such an impelling need, the overwhelming majority of novelists between the 1830s and the 1880s accepted the solution proposed by Alessandro Manzoni's masterpiece, *The Betrothed.* The issue, in so far as they were concerned, was not solely artistic but one that had to be viewed in the context of the country's efforts to achieve political unity. Post-*Risorgimento* novelists, on the other hand, insisted on and enjoyed a greater stylistic elasticity. They made use of regional terms or, as in Verga's case, strove to fashion a language which, while phonetically understandable by the general reader, irrespective of his birthplace in the peninsula, conveyed through its structure the flavor of the uniqueness and diversity of the characters of a novel.

Social themes, a simpler language and, last but not least, objectivity of treatment became the cornerstones of *verismo* whose impact continued to be felt by the generations of writers who followed Capuana and Verga.

By and large, in Giulio Cattaneo's words, the novelists of the second half of the century "were not, politically speaking, revolutionaries. In many cases, they were guided, or at least they so believed, by humanitarian intentions." What distinguished them from their predecessors is not only what they saw and understood about life but the manner in which they translated their perceptions into literature. Thus, for example, the *veristi* painted a picture, usually dismal, of life and affirmed: "*This is reality.*" Beginning with Svevo and Pirandello, however, the question seemed to have remained the same, but the emphasis had changed to "Is *this* reality?" The dramatic shift from *parti pris* to a position pregnant with metaphysical and psychological implications required stylistic and structural changes—so clearly visible in the work of Svevo and Pirandello: the former substituted psychological order for the traditional chronological or historical order most of his predecessors and contemporaries observed; the latter, after having written several structurally conventional novels, boldly abandoned the tradition. His *Uno, nessuno e centomila* (1926; *One, None and a Hundred Thousand*, N.Y., 1933) is divided into one hundred brief chapters, a structure that dramatically underscores the fragmentation of the ordinary life of an ordinary person—and by doing so, Pirandello gave the genre a dimension of flexibility and unconventionality we recognize as two of the chief features of the novel of today.

There are many other differences between the novels of the *Risorgimento* and those of post-Unification Italy. As generally conceived in the early part of the nineteenth century, the novel had primarily been concerned with man and society, with the development of the individual striving to fulfill himself as a spiritual and social being. On the whole, the hero of such novels was buffeted by outside forces and frequently found himself at odds with the social order in which he existed. The effect and interest of such novels depended largely on the story itself, the intricacies and suspense generated by the plot, the credibility of its climate and milieu recreated by the artist, the manner in which the author was able to define and resolve the moral, spiritual, and sociopolitical conflicts between his characters or between some of the characters and their society. In the end, the reader could count on finding himself substantially instructed by the "message," or the lesson implicit in the story. ("I've learnt," says Renzo in the final page of Manzoni's *The Betrothed*, "not to get into riots; I've learnt not to make speeches in the street; I've learnt not to raise my elbow too much . . ." and so forth.) The novels of the *veristi* and their followers urged a more objective presentation of the facts, circumstances, and characters of their stories, leaving it up to the reader to decide for himself according to his standards and values the ramifications and consequences of good and evil. The traditional hero of the early decades of the nineteenth century had a special dimension: he learned and matured as he lived, and his character was slowly molded by his experience. And in this sense there is no question that there is something reassuring about Manzoni's Renzo and Lucia, for example, who live in a well-structured society where the line of separation between good and evil is generally extremely clear. Similarly, we are confident and secure in the novels of the *veristi* where the characters enjoy an unparalleled amount of autonomy, and where we do not fail to see the relationships between one character and another, and between them and society: the writer has become invisible, no longer manipulating his characters and events for his own specific reasons.

The changing social and political situation in Italy toward the end of the nineteenth century, as well as a retreat to more conservative positions of aesthetics, brought about the demise of *verismo*. If, on the one hand, many readers and critics had welcomed a less inhibited treatment

of social and psychological themes in forms less bound by
conventions, others came to resent the fact the veristic
novels had generally focused on the less inviting, not to say
seamy, sides of life—the squalor of poverty, the misery of
the exploited, the human capacity to engage in debasing,
immoral and revolting acts—that tended to forge a definitely unfavorable image of Italy. The reaction against
verismo with all its intensity and vituperativeness was a
political as well as an artistic event. It was led by those who
fought the democratization of political life in Italy as well
as by those who felt personally offended by the message of
the new fiction. The polemics became more vociferous and
bitter as the century came to a close. One of the most reactionary of such critics, Enrico A. Butti, asked: "What have
we got from the past fifty years? Imitators of Manzoni and
the *veristi*. The former are already dead. . . . the others
were nothing if not imitators of French naturalism." Most
critics had not missed the connection between *verismo* and
the changed political climate and were eager to exploit this
fact whenever possible. What they stubbornly refused to
acknowledge is that one of the traditional functions of
literature has been to question, seriously and honestly, the
moral values of a civilization at a particular historical moment. In this sense Italy was in fact in step with France,
England, and the Scandinavian countries. Everywhere, it
seemed, writers were addressing themselves to issues of
great social and ethical relevance: the rampant spiritual
corruption, viewed particularly through the varying standards people would espouse according to the problem facing
them; the demeaning condition of the women; the squalid
character of city life; and the almost hopelessness of rural
life. The political and cultural Establishment did not find
such themes palatable, for they implicitly entailed an objective reappraisal of the values that are the root causes of
human problems.

The reaction against *verismo* notwithstanding, the validity of the ethics of a social system continued to be challenged in one form or another. True enough, Gabriele
d'Annunzio continued to busy himself with novels depicting

the rather glorious but meaningless existence of his beautiful people, while Serao, after finishing a number of impressive novels in the tradition of *verismo*, began making pious remarks about the solace religion could bring to the less fortunate members of society. Economic and social success —two aspirations of bourgeois thinking—were looked at from a less sympathetic point of view: Verga had questioned the true importance of such a yardstick in the face of defeat man ultimately experiences in the hands of fate. Now Pirandello began dealing with the irreconcilability of the individual and his society. A few years later, Italo Svevo was to dramatize the futility of and the impredictability of success by showing how Zeno, the hero of *The Confessions of Zeno*, becomes enormously successful despite his bungling and inept handling of his affairs.

By and large, the literary scene between the *fin de siècle* and the 1910s proved to be notably conservative. The only movement that could be called radical was futurism, characterized by Sergio Antonielli as a "movement that called past, a past to be ignored and destroyed, every thing that had taken place before the date of its manifestoes [1909]." The Italian novel itself lost much of its popularity and prestige in its home ground, while the French and Russian acquired new influence. The cultivated readers and critics responded to poetry, thanks particularly to the great "Triad" —Carducci, Pascoli and d'Annunzio—exalted and praised as the poets of the "third" Italy. The mood and intellectual climate of the period under scrutiny was one of confusion and indecisiveness. "Individualism," noted Giuseppe Petronio, "the flight from reality, spiritualism, activism [and] a timid withdrawal to the self become the dominating characteristics of the period." The decadent mysticism of Antonio Fogazzaro, the exceptional egocentricity of d'Annunzio, the pale lyrics of the so-called "Crepuscolari" poets (poets of the "Twilight"), and the novels of Svevo, Pirandello, and Borgese mirror the restlessness, anxiety and sense of loss of a period Francesco Flora dubbed "of historical perplexity."

Svevo and Pirandello once again proved to be subversive

novelists in the sense that they changed the rules of the game. Their point of departure was *verismo* and naturalism, to be sure. But while placing the action of their tales in a recognizable regional milieu (Trieste and Rome or Sicily respectively), they focused not on the practical but on the metaphysical predicament of their characters, stressing not the certainties (*il vero*, as it were) of life, but its paradoxes and inconclusiveness. Such inconclusiveness, far from being an artistic deficiency, is an accurate reflection of the disintegration of values that was, and has continued to be a reality of our own time. Both Svevo and Pirandello produced a far less structured vision of a world, and their work signals a turning inward to discover in the self the real factors that produce the external chaos.

The aesthetics of Benedetto Croce and his views on literature (ranging all the way from his rejection of the legitimacy of literary genres to his definition of art as intuition), whatever his intentions might have been, placed a higher premium on poetry, a far "purer" creative activity than the novel, with the result that poetry regained some of the prestige it had lost to fiction.

The role played by the many magazines that sprang up in Florence at the turn of the century vis-à-vis the fate of the novel in Italy remains to be determined. What can be said in this context is that the policy of such reviews did much to consign the novel to a lesser position in the literary hierarchy. *La Voce*, edited first by a restless, self-taught young man, Giuseppe Prezzolini, and then by Giuseppe De Robertis, played a central role in introducing poets from other nations. It published, frequently for the first time, many of the future masters of Italian poetry, Umberto Saba and Giuseppe Ungaretti among them. Prezzolini embraced completely Croce's aesthetics, as he himself was to acknowledge when he wrote: "Many of us [of *La Voce*] considered art as a lyrical effort, and it seemed to us that a lyrical effort could not last long. . . . it seemed to us that in this [respect] we were following one of the clearest and [most] arousing directives of Croce. And we went on searching for lyrical passages or moments of an author, considering the rest a connecting fabric, a labor of rhetoric or pedagogy or of patience. . . . In sum, *La Voce* for many [people] is still tied to this attempt to reduce poetic inspiration to a moment of *purity*, in which there is no mixing of morality or practicality or eloquence."

Prezzolini's special quest for truth as he called it was to lead many of the influential critics of the time to point out that truth could be equated only with autobiography, the only truth a writer presumably knows—a stance that explains the pervasively autobiographical character of literature in Italy for a good part of the early decades of this century. Similarly, the espousal of the concept of the brief nature of poetic inspiration also accounts for the devotion to, and attention enjoyed by the so-called *frammento*, or prose poem, a new genre practised with unusual craftsmanship and brilliancy by Emilio Cecchi, a Crocean and a vocal critic of the novel. In another city, Rome, the influential magazine *La Ronda* (1919–23), edited by Cecchi himself, Antonio Baldini, Vincenzo Cardarelli, and two less-known artists, proposed a return to the tradition of Italian classical poetry as exemplified by Petrarch, Leopardi, and Manzoni, and openly encouraged an emulation of their work. Hailing the purity of poetry, the new arbiters of public literary taste engaged in what one critic, Giacomo Debenedetti, has aptly called "an antinovel program." In such circumstances, it was inevitable that such a polymorphic genre as the novel would have more than its share of problems. Much as the novel suffered from a discouraging lack of interest, it could still count on a limited number of *aficionados*. Of these, the most enthusiastic and optimistic was Giuseppe A. Borgese, a learned scholar of broad intellectual interests, ranging all the way from aesthetics to fiction and poetry. The numerous reviews and articles he published in a variety of dailies and magazines developed a theme particularly dear to his heart: the time had come "to build," as he put it (the title of one of his collections of reviews and essays is precisely *Tempo di edificare* [Time to build]), a term that for him meant devoting one's own creative energies to writing fiction.

Borgese's critical activism was certainly welcomed and needed, particularly at a time when *la belle page* was having its day. Despite the presence of d'Annunzio, Fogazzaro, and Pirandello, the Italian literary scene was distinguished by an upsurge of poetry, prose poems, and the sensitive, autobiographical works of a group of writers frequently called *moralists*: Giovanni Boine (1887–1917), Carlo Michelstaedter (1887–1910), Piero Jahier (1884–1966), and Scipio Slataper (1888–1915). By the end of World War I, the novel was on its way back. The new period was marked, as Giacomo Debenedetti writes, "by a receptiveness on the part of critics and readers toward the novel understood as a work of art, and as a human and moral message." Only then, he continues, "did Italian writers experience a new relish to write novels," almost as if the writers who had reached maturity "were forced, or at least brought to the point of reinventing the genre of the novel in Italy, recreating it with all the chrisms of what in those days was considered good, serious, cultivated, responsible literature." That moment has been located in 1920–21, during which several of Tozzi's novels appeared, one of them after the death of the writer. A few years later, Alberto Moravia would publish at his own expense *Gli indifferenti* (1929; *The Time of Indifference*, N.Y., 1953). And with that work, a new chapter in the history of the novel in Italy would begin.

2

Luigi Capuana: The Theorist as Novelist

One of the anomalies of Italian literature is that an imposing number of its most significant intellectuals come from the depressed area called the *Mezzogiorno,* which includes that part of the peninsula that stretches all the way from south of Rome to the tip of the boot, and includes the islands of Sicily and Sardinia. Until recent times, the *Mezzogiorno* was primarily agricultural in terms of economics and monarchical-fascistic in terms of its politics. Neglected for centuries, a semicolonial state often ignored by the central government when Italy became independent, ridiculed for its conservative life style and its reactionary politics by the freer, less inhibited north, the south has nevertheless made a substantial contribution to the culture of Italy. From the earliest times of Italian civilization (the famous and influential court of Frederick II) throughout the Renaissance (Tasso, Giordano Bruno, Sannazzaro, and Marino) to modern times (Vico, De Sanctis, Croce, Verga, Pirandello, Deledda, and Quasimodo), the south has been the birthplace of eminent philosophers, sensitive poets and powerful novelists. In every case the legacy of southern culture can be felt, with different intensity, in the works of philosophy and fiction alike of its native sons, who exhibit a skepticism toward the effectiveness and honesty of any government, a deep-rooted distrust of those who live in what the Sicilians, with a mixture of awe, envy, and resentment, call *il continente* ("the mainland")—a term that dramatizes the feeling of estrangement felt by the majority of southerners. Life in the often barren regions of the south, the poverty of its soil and, until recent times at least, its prevalently agricultural-feudal economy have traditionally sharpened the writer's awareness of the plight of his *paesani*. Living an almost hopeless existence, without much opportunity to improve one's standard of living, is a tragic but normal fact of life in the *Mezzogiorno*. It is not enough, however, to be born in the south and to be endowed with certain creative qualities to write about the south. The roots in one's own soil and culture are always better understood when one lives in places radically different from one's native town. And for this reason alone we perceive that almost without exception the southern writer "found" himself and produced his best work only after he returned home from a self-imposed exile that permitted him to taste life in other, perhaps culturally more exciting, cities. This is true of De Sanctis (one of the towering intellects of modern Italian culture), Verga, Pirandello, Quasimodo, and Vittorini—the first and most famous names that come immediately to mind—as it is with Luigi Capuana. Another feature that seems to be common to the great majority of the so-called southern writers is the philosophical and critical component of their activity as intellectuals. It is hard to find a fine writer from the south who has not made some impact with his criticism even when, as in the case of Pirandello, his noncreative work was savagely attacked by the professional critics in the Establishment or, as in the case of Quasimodo, it was not widely read and understood. Certainly it is in the group of writers-critics that Luigi Capuana may rightfully be said to belong. Throughout his long and productive life, he displayed an admirable capacity to be an attentive critic, a perceptive theorist of literature, as well as an able practitioner of several literary genres.

Luigi Capuana was born in Mineo, near Catania, on May 28, 1839, the first of eight children and, as Luigi Tonelli remarked, "having lived between 1839 and 1915, in a singularly important and eventful time in Italian political and literary history, from his early youth [and] throughout the rest of his life, [he] was never absent from the political and cultural life [of his nation]." No characterization of Capuana could be fairer: he was both a thinker and a doer, constantly involved in shaping his country's culture, working to give it a breadth and sophistication consonant with the image of the "new," united Italy. One example may suffice to indicate Capuana's modernity: "Art does not have a special function: its first duty is to be art, nothing else." Few readers of today would find such a statement unusual, for the fundamental "uselessness" of art in general, and literature in particular, is widely accepted as a basic tenet of contemporary aesthetics. But in Capuana's times the concept of "art-for-art's sake" was controversial and opposed, particularly by those who recognized the effectiveness with which the novel, and to a more limited extent poetry, had shown its capacity to translate into an artistic form the patriotic and religious duties of civilized man. In post-*Risorgimento* Italy, the novel was turned into a powerful tool to bring the readers to a confrontation with social inequities no longer tolerable by a presumably free nation.

Capuana, a loyal and patriotic man, became one of the few intellectuals who questioned the assumptions of such a view of literature. He was also one of the minds receptive to new ideas and new concepts of the novel, a perfectly good reason why today he is remembered not only for the books of fiction he wrote with great profusion, but for the role he played as the architect of *verismo* and as its most articulate spokesman.

In many ways, the life, upbringing, and education of Capuana unmistakably point to the typical intellectual trajectory of a southerner: an education in a good, often private school and enrollment in a school of jurisprudence with the aim of a law degree. Politically, he seems to have been far more liberal than his countrymen, imbued as he was with a patriotism that was genuinely militant. When he began to feel that the climate of his native city was beginning to be too restrictive, he followed in the footsteps of many other Sicilians, and left for the north—Florence and Milan. The multifarious activities which engaged his talent furnish ample proof of vitality and diversity. He showed his serious commitment to literature, and his early work is indicative of an inquiring mind, broad interests, and urbanity of views. He spent four productive years in Florence (1864–68), making friends with writers and intellectuals and working as theatre critic for the newspaper *La nazione*. It was a rich, valuable apprenticeship, for it afforded him with the opportunity of acquainting himself with several other literatures, particularly the French. In 1869 his health forced his return to Sicily, where he spent seven years continuing his readings, this time in the area of philosophy and aesthetics, especially Hegel, De Sanctis, and De Meis. Back in Milan in 1877, he became a contributor to *Il corriere della sera* and the prestigious review *La nuova antologia*. In Milan he had the good fortune of meeting a fellow Sicilian, Giovanni Verga, who soon became his best friend. Their friendship was to prove very important when Verga published his first great novel, *I Malavoglia*, a work strenuously and effectively praised by Capuana. His own publications appeared regularly: *Profili di donne* (1877), a collection of short stories; critical essays, *Il teatro italiano contemporaneo* (1877); *Studi sulla letteratura contemporanea* (1880 aand 1882); fairy tales (*C'era una volta . . .* 1882); and his first novel, *Giacinta* (1879) which, together with *Il marchese di Roccaverdina* (1910), are considered choice Capuana.

In 1882 he was appointed Professor of Italian at the Womens' Teachers College in Rome, and in 1902, Professor of Lexicography and Stylistics at the University of Catania. He seems to have taken his duties lightly, however, thus leaving himself open to the attacks of some of his more vitriolic critics, who remarked sarcastically that the University had produced several fine critics during his tenure, thanks to the fact that he was there so seldom!

In 1911 the city of Catania celebrated the seventieth birthday of one of its more illustrious citizens. Four years later, on November 29, 1915, he died.

Unquestionably, Capuana's sojourn in the north was of inestimable importance, particularly in terms of his exposure to foreign literatures. His own work as a theatre critic conveys the dissatisfaction he felt with the artificiality and sentimentalism pervading much of Romanticism—dissatisfaction that prodded him to demand that plays be less contrived, closer to real life. By the same token, the work he read of such novelists as Balzac and Zola persuaded him that literature should be open to scabrous social, psychological, and moral problems long hidden under the rug. His conviction got him into difficulties when he published *Giacinta*, a work many of his contemporaries, including even his loyal friend Giovanni Verga, found in part unnecessarily controversial.

Capuana's commitment to literature is characterized by his dual role: from the beginning of his career, he was absorbed by what makes literature enduring and important and focused on close-range studies of the artist's technique, with particular attention to the architecture of a literary work. Writing always challenged him, and through an active practise of the craft he sharpened his own critical perception. At times his role as a critic diminished his effectiveness as a creative artist. Yet, the particular nature of his interests never inhibited him from posing questions regarding the validity of traditional themes and structures. On the contrary, he sought to embody in his fiction some of the theories he discussed and defended in his writings. In his critical pronouncements and in his theoretical papers one feels less the presence of a highly speculative mind, trained in the stringent logic of philosophy and aesthetics, or that of a ground-breaking innovator, than that of an alert, sensitive person ready to recognize, at times anticipate and support the inevitable changes taking place when a literary tradition evolves. Such changes were part and parcel of a fundamentally new way to look at reality squarely and honestly, all the time searching for a style that was to be "lively, effective, and capable of portraying all the imperceptible nuances of modern thought." In this respect, Capuana unmistakably called for nothing less than a revolt against the conservative, unimaginative positions of the cultural establishment, traditionally overcautious in the sensitive area of the literary language. "Our masters did nothing but advise us to read the writers of the fourteenth century. We needed an easy, vigorous, dramatic language, and our teachers suggested that we read the playwrights of the sixteenth century." Here again Capuana was in the avant-garde when he insisted that "the present time of Italian life" should be, if not the exclusive, at least a top-priority concern of the writers—an advice, incidentally, heeded by a substantial number of novelists, playwrights, and poets including Serao, Di Giacomo, Verga, Deledda, Pirandello, and the early d'Annunzio. The time was ripe to begin looking at reality as it was and not as the writer would like it to be. The time was at hand when the artist would grapple with human instincts, passions, and problems without fearing that his readers would be shocked or repelled.

Capuana did not reach these conclusions independently. In the closing pages of his brilliant *History of Italian Literature*, Francesco De Sanctis (one of Capuana's favorite critics) had written *à propos* of a new literature for a modern Italy:

> To create such a literature . . . two conditions are indispensable. The first is serious study of the whole range of knowledge, guided by a spirit of patiently exploring criticism, entirely free and unprejudiced. The second is a national life, both public and private, developed over a long period. Let us look into our hearts . . . let us look into our customs, ideas, and prejudices, our qualities both good and bad; let us seize on this modern world and make it our own, by studying, assimilating, and transforming it . . . We are still enmeshed in the academy and arcadia, in classicism and romanticisms, and are not yet free from the vices of emphasis and rhetoric, those signs of a want of seriousness in life and in study. From our very boastings can be seen the sense of our own inferiority. [Trans. Joan Redfern (New York: Basic Books, 1931), 2:946–47]

De Sanctis's proddings must, of course, be understood in the context of post-*Risorgimento* Italian history. For it became increasingly clear to the creative artists that the climate was ripe for a dramatic change from an idealized view of reality to a more cogent and profound understanding of it. This is why the first national trend to emerge in a country united at last should be *verismo*, a term that by itself underscored its commitment to *verità*, truth, to a depiction of the way things really were. The turn literature took was both inevitable and salutary: for if the country really intended to know herself, her writers would have to begin with the places and the life they knew best, their regions and their towns—something that explains why the bulk of the most significant fiction written in Italy from the mid-1870s to the end of the century was regionalistic in content and realistic in form. Thus, the writers of Romanticism had worked "on spiritual experiences and, less burdened by the sense of the relative, created a national spirit . . . the *veristi* on the other hand, loved Italy [through] their own regions and their own dialects, and, looking at exterior facts —customs, landscape, nature—successfully seized her characteristics," as Giulio Marzot remarks. Capuana proved to be correct when he affirmed that *verismo* was nothing if not a "technique," although I would also add a "state of mind." Whatever its flaws, whatever its limitations and incorrect premises, one thing became certain: after *verismo* Italian literature, and the novel in particular, would never be the same.

During his long critical activity, Capuana's concept of art underwent inevitable changes. But he remained always true to the two basic pillars of his stance: sincerity and impersonality. By the former he meant a commitment to truth as the artist saw it, depicted honestly and fairly. By the latter he meant the absolute necessity for the writer to be absent, invisible as it were, from his stories, withholding judgments about his characters and actions, since such judgments should be made by the reader himself. The writer, he advised, should "forget, obliterate himself," and allow the creatures of his imagination live an autonomous life. Perfection in art, for Capuana, was closely tied to the principle of impersonality: "once the writer had found the right subject," as Vincenzo Traversa notes in his study of Capuana, "and [once] he had inspired life into his characters, he had to leave them free to play their own role, without intervening in one way or another. . . . the writer's greatness reached its highest level when, standing aside, he allowed his characters to play their parts, free of following their impulses, their 'tragic fate.'"

We are aware, of course, of the fact that, strictly speaking, there is not, nor can there ever be a truly "impersonal art." Books are written by people—people with passions, ambitions, hopes, dreams, anxieties—and it is only very rarely that a writer can completely objectify these and other feelings and experiences. Moreover, as Croce himself remarked in his essay on Capuana, such impersonal art "would have to be [one] that neither laughs nor cries, that does not allow likes or dislikes to leak out, that does not color its own representations passionately or sentimentally. . . ." Such art, continues Croce, "has never existed and will never exist." It is doubtful that the contemporary reader can accept the finality of such a statement. Capuana certainly meant a rejection of an author-narrator-protagonist identification that was widespread in romantic literature to the point of damaging, if not completely destroying, the credibility of fiction.

If in terms of his special interest in psychology and the sciences, Capuana's position in his own literature was unorthodox, it can hardly be said that on the whole he operated in a vacuum. The ties that linked him with his literary tradition in general, and certain novelists in particular, were quite strong. With De Marchi, for example, he believed that the artist should strive to portray contemporary reality; with Verga, Di Giacomo, and Serao he was convinced that a novelist should draw his inspiration from the cities and provinces alike, the one prerequisite being that the incidents be narrated in such a way as to have a strong flavor of historical authenticity. In his view, the regional novel would eventually lead to a national novel and then become, in fact, "more regional, so as to give its creations the same variety and richness of Nature's creation."

Capuana's links with European literature are best illustrated by his unquestionable awareness of the importance of psychology, which would give an added dimension to the scope of fiction. Without accepting all of Zola's tenets, especially his systematic, quasiscientific approach in the structural planning of the novels of the cycle *Les Rougon-Maquarts*, he emphasized the importance of what he called "the human document," in *Studii sulla letteratura italiana*. "We must start off from the human document, in order to reconstruct the psychological process that has taken place. . . . we must begin with the symptoms in order to understand the kind of illness involved, and whether it is included among those already known and described in scientific manuals and journals."

For all the boldness and visionary quality of his views on the form and fate of the novel, however, Capuana showed little propensity for linguistic experimentation. He applauded the geniality of Verga's stylistic solution realized in *I Malavoglia*, but contented himself with making his own characters speak a literary language appropriate to their surroundings and social conditions. In a climate of stylistic renewal and rejuvenation, of exciting and often fruitful attempts to restudy the problems of fiction, Capuana maintained that feelings and characters, no matter how well portrayed, would in themselves no longer be sufficient to justify a work of art. He urged the writer to use the initial incident of his tale as a springboard for a patient, careful reconstruction of the antecedents, motivations, and background of the central events. By means of such reconstruction, he hoped to find if not the precise answer at least a clue to the mystery of human actions. Much of his fiction bears impressive evidence of his attempt to discover, through his analyses of human neuroses and mental illnesses, the reasons for anormal or abnormal behavior.

Capuana's criticism, as Giulio Marzot suggests in his study of the *Ottocento* and *verismo*, "helps us clarify the writer and vice versa." Capuana's first novel, *Giacinta*, has the specific ingredients advocated by the theoretical premises of *verismo*: its plot set in the present in an undisclosed but obviously provincial milieu on the Adriatic coast; it is written in a genuinely simple style and is constructed in a manner calculated to carry out in a carefully documented way the history of the crisis of an individual and, by extension, of a particular segment of society. The whole story revolves around the protagonist whose name is the book's title. The author's major task is to show how her corruption, degradation, and tragic end are to be seen and understood both in the context of her personal, private events and of certain sociological conditions.

Giacinta, the only child of the middle-class family of the Merulli, is raised by a nurse in the country. "Her coming into the world had not been a source of great pleasure for her mother." Her father is an inept minor civil servant; her mother is an unhappy, greedy, and as we soon discover, promiscuous woman, intent only in increasing the family's modest fortune. When still a little girl, Giacinta is raped by a fourteen-year-old waif, Beppe, her only male playmate. In order to hide the tragic happening from the townspeople, Giacinta is sent away to a boarding school, while her servant Camilla and Beppe are dismissed from the household. Several years later Giacinta, now a young lady approaching the age of marriage, comes back home to find the main floor of her home transformed into the office of the Agricultural Bank, whose director, Signor Commendatore Saviani, lives with the family, having become one of her mother's lovers. Longing for affection and understanding, Giacinta finds neither from her parents. One day, quite accidentally, she reexperiences in her mind the traumatic loss of her virginity as a child. The horror that had never been fully realized is now perceived in its full extent. The revelation comes at a critical moment in her development as a human being and nearly destroys her: she falls ill with typhus and goes through a long, painful convalescence. The illness sharpens her sensitivity: she realizes the corruption of her mother (who enjoys the favors of Giacinta's young friends), the weakness of her father, the degradation of the society in which she lives; she also realizes that she is an attractive young woman, admired and courted by old and young men alike.

Giacinta's past haunts her and takes the twin form of a

self-destructive impulse and a growing feeling of estrangement from her mother and father: she suffers of an incapacity to identify with someone she respects and loves. Indeed, it is such a negative feeling that leads her to refuse to
conform to prevailing social-moral norms. Of the many
suitors she has, she falls in love with Andrea Gerace, a
minor bank employee who sang at one of the parties given
by her family to celebrate the end of her convalescence. But
their love is unrequieted because of the psychological elements involved. Giacinta's loss of virginity, considered by
her society a factor that destroys the integrity and dignity of
a woman, together with the lack of strong ties with her
parents, make her feel like an outcast. By the moral standards of her society she is undesirable, sinful, impure, and
therefore unworthy of a normal marriage.

Suddenly, an important event alters an already complex
situation: Giacinta finds herself the heiress of a large fortune (some three hundred thousand lire in government
bonds) bequeathed her by a cousin who has died in Paris.
The inheritance proves to be a bag of mixed blessings: while
it does make Giacinta freer from her repressive, domineer-
ing mother, it is hated by Andrea who accepted Giacinta
for what she was, not for what she possessed. Feeling unworthy of Andrea, Giacinta decides to marry Giulio Grippa
di San Gelso, an aging, prematurely senile count who accepts the terms of the marriage imposed by his wife: he is
to live with Giacinta as if he were her brother, not her husband. Andrea becomes Giacinta's lover, a kind of paramour-
in-residence, and fathers the child born from their union, a
little girl named Adelina.

The scandalous affair between the two must not be permitted to continue, lest the whole family be censured by
the community. But when Giacinta's mother tries to have
Andrea transferred to Sicily, Giacinta pledges to support
him even though her act, however generous, proves to be
one more item contributing to his loss of freedom and self-
respect.

After six years their love is tested first by the sudden
death by diptheria of their child, then by the deplorable

state in which Andrea finds himself, living like a worm at the feet of his mistress. The world the two had so precariously built together is fast crumbling. The failing health of the old count and of Giacinta's father, capped by Giacinta's mother's acceptance of an immoral situation, robs the two lovers of the very reason for being together. A sinful relation breeds boredom and dissatisfaction once it is tolerated by society. Having first lost her child and then Andrea, nothing is left to Giacinta but to commit the last act of self-destruction, and she takes her own life with poison.

Although the novel occasionally suffers from being over-dramatic, it certainly ranks as an impressive piece of writing in the naturalist vein in Italy, particularly as an engrossing attempt to show the conspicuous role heredity and environment play in molding the character and life of an individual. The case study is meticulously developed by Capuana: Giacinta's mother is persuasive as a calculating, perfidious, and vulgar woman who will stop at nothing when her material well-being and personal vanity are concerned; her husband is excellently, though briefly, depicted as innocuous as a partner and ineffectual as a father. The society in which the story unfolds and in which the two protagonists live is callous, however much it tries to conceal its immorality and greed behind a façade of bourgeois respectability. Giulio and Andrea are little more than clowns or fools in acceding to perform their part at the tune of the heroine's music. And the language, although at times a little too literary, effectively translates onto the printed page the emotions of its characters and the events in which they are involved.

If the plot itself is hardly original (it owes much to Flaubert's *Madame Bovary* and, to a lesser extent, to Balzac and Zola), the manner in which it is told—the structure of the book, as it were—represents an original departure from conventional technique. As E. A. Walker recently underscored, the story does not unfold chronologically, as the reader may have assumed from my brief synopsis, but by means of flashbacks. The book opens with the flirtations being enjoyed by the heroine, admired and much sought-after, but quickly moves back to the past searching for the antecedents of Giacinta's situation. Much like Verga's *I Malavoglia* the author does not indulge in descriptions of his characters: his purpose is to lead the reader to recognize and penetrate, unaided by the author, the *personae* of the book. Having introduced us to the story, Capuana takes us back in time and carefully re-creates the disturbing elements in Giacinta's childhood that have contributed to her tragic situation. Yet from the very beginning two elements emerge most strikingly: the thoroughly degrading milieu in which the heroine lives and the meaningless, empty rapport between Giacinta and her mother and father. That both elements are essential to our understanding of the book can hardly be disputed: is not Giacinta, after all, engaged in what amounts to nothing less than a concerted, conscious attempt to reject the vulgar values and false standards of her society by her outrageously noncomformist behavior? And is not she also engaged, though not altogether consciously, in a process of self-destruction rooted in her parents' rejection of her as a human being and as their child?

Il Marchese di Roccaverdina surely ranks as Capuana's best novel. Composed almost a quarter of a century after *Giacinta*, the work is free of the theoretical preoccupation and the stylistic excesses that occasionally mar the earlier novel. It is also less concerned with proving its point (i.e., the documented manner in which a woman of good stock degrades herself through a combination of hereditary and environmental causes), than with dealing seriously and profoundly with the more universal problem of human guilt.

Linear in construction, sober and even terse in style, *Il Marchese di Roccaverdina* revolves around a single, Hamletian question: can an individual responsible for having committed the crime of murder be able to live with his conscience, even when circumstances permit him to go unpunished? The corollary question is: just how and for how long does a human being have to pay for his crime?

The story begins *in medias res*: a man has been murdered. His name is Rocco Criscione. The questions are: who killed him? Is it his wife Agrippina Solmo, or Neli Casaccio, who is known to have threatened Rocco upon learning that he was making advances to his wife? Or did someone else commit the crime? What motivated the murder? Was it Agrippina's jealousy, or revenge on Neli's part? Circumstantial evidence seems to indicate irrefutably that Neli is the murderer: not only was he known to be Rocco's enemy, but he was also seen in the general area where the crime was committed. Neli has no alibi: in view of the evidence, he is assumed to be guilty and is sentenced to a fifteen-year term in prison.

The truth is quite different, as we learn in the second chapter. The marquis, not Neli, is the murderer. The motive is jealousy. For over ten years, Agrippina had been the marquis's servant and mistress. Conscious of local traditions and the Sicilian code of honor, the marquis had arranged a marriage between Agrippina and Rocco, a trusted farmhand, on condition that the two would not live as man and wife. Grown suspicious that the arrangement was not being honored (a suspicion confirmed only later in the story), the marquis ambushed Rocco and killed him. The affair is by no means over, however, for the marquis begins feeling remorse for what he has done. Unable to live with his conscience, he seeks the help of the town priest, don Silvio, a humble and charitable man. Don Silvio's religion—and particularly his vow to secrecy in the confessional—prevent him from putting the matter to rights: all he can do is to try, without success, persuading the real culprit to go to the authorities and confess the truth.

Meanwhile, the marquis is feeling the pressure of his aunt, the Baroness of Lagomorto, and of his aging nursemaid, Grazia, to marry so that the family name will be carried on and his property be protected. The candidate for the marriage is a Zosima Mugnos, a woman with whom the marquis had been in love many years earlier, and who now has almost resigned herself to be a spinster and live the rest of her life in dignified poverty with her mother and sister. The marquis is well disposed toward her and promises that the marriage will take place after the end of a ten-month drought that has severely jeopardized the year's harvests.

The drought is broken at last, and the people are overjoyed. But the marriage is delayed further. The marquis attempts to forget the horrible crime he has committed: he has confessed it, to be sure, but has not really repented. To ease his conscience, he engages in exemplary work of charity, donates to the church a beautiful but troubling cross with Christ; runs for political office (only to turn down the enthusiastic councilmen's nomination to mayor on the grounds that he is too busy), and forms a farmers' cooperative aimed at increasing the efficiency, the quality, and the technology in the production of local wines. Nothing seems to help his troubled mind, however: not charity, not business, not politics, and not even his eventual marriage with Zosima, who feels unloved by her husband and threatened by the "presence" of Agrippina. Life itself seems to persecute him: Neli Casaccio's widow implores him to employ her son so that the family will not starve (he refuses, but Zosima complies with the poor woman's request); Santi Dimaura, a poor devil who has been forced by the marquis to sell him his land for a pittance, is found hanging from a tree on the property that at one time belonged to him; don Acquilante Guzzardi, a lawyer with a propensity for experimenting with witchcraft (claiming that only by asking the dead can one learn the guilt of the living), seems unconvinced by the results of the investigation. The passing of time is equally of no help. Don Silvio has died, and so has Neli, who took his own life in prison declaring his innocence. The two people directly involved in the awful incident can no longer threaten the criminal. And still nothing helps. No longer able to go on coping with his troubled conscience by repressing the haunting awareness of his crime, the marquis runs to the spot where Rocco had been found, and unloads his gun. Rapidly he becomes insane: his confused words reveal to everyone what no one had dared think: the marquis is the sole person responsible for the tragedy and death that have destroyed the lives of several innocent people. Zosima leaves him in despair, and Agrippina returns for a while to take care of the madman. As the book comes to a close, we know that the marquis' hours are counted.

The book is, simply stated, about crime and punishment. But it is also more than that: it is a scorching, if indirect, indictment of a social order that permits killers to go unpunished while innocent people are jailed; it is a low-keyed commentary on the various types of manipulations and exploitations—human, social, economic, and political—of the peasantry by the landowners. And, through a strategic conversion of certain sides of the novel into symbols, the work attains greater relevance. Thus, for example, the parched soil we see at the beginning of the book may be what T. S. Eliot would have called the "objective correlative," the object that reflects and reveals the spiritual character of the hero of the story; the rain that breaks the damning, destructive drought may be seen as God's tears over the crimes of His children (the episode recalls the end of the pestilence in Alessandro Manzoni's *I promessi sposi*); Agrippina's humility and true love, so different from the pathetic, weak, and resigned love of Zosima, come close to that Love that alone can be Charity, love unrewarded, unselfishly given no matter what the circumstances.

Il Marchese di Roccaverdina is particularly keen in its depiction of a world of violence, intrigues, jealousy, remorse, rapaciousness. In a world such as the one Capuana presents, it is problematical for compassion and justice for one's neighbor to exist, except sporadically and in the most unusual circumstances. Ultimately we must agree that the real theme of the book is man's cruelty, his lust, his egocentricity and selfishness, his constant but unsuccessful attempts to silence the voice of his conscience. And one of Capuana's most important achievements is to have placed his knowledge of local conditions not at the service of folklore, but at the service of his efforts to illuminate further the secret ways of human passions.

3

Gabriele d'Annunzio: The Birth of Superman

Whatever opinion readers and critics may have about Gabriele d'Annunzio, he is unquestionably one of the most controversial and most discussed literary personalities of modern Italian culture. In the early years of this century, Benedetto Croce put it clearly when he wrote: "It is beyond doubt that d'Annunzio occupies a large place in the modern soul and that, as a consequence, he will occupy [a similar place] in the histories that will be written about the spiritual life of our time." Certainly few other poets dominated the world of letters, and perhaps even fewer lived a life as daring, damning, and dramatic as he: poet premature at the age of sixteen, novelist of repute, scenario writer (he was among the very first novelists to become aware of the possibilities of the new medium), soldier, flier, political figure, polemicist, d'Annunzio lived a life full of scandals of most kinds—personal, financial, military, diplomatic, and political—all of which certainly helped to draw interest to his work. He was, this much is sure, a man of genius, of exceptional vanity and versatility, who had an uncanny ability to catch and retain public attention with a flair today's Madison Avenue advertising agencies could justifiably envy. In the words of the anonymous reviewer of the *Times Literary Supplement*, December 29, 1966:

> In the role of cultural fugleman to his country he was helped and not hindered by his extravagance of manner. That as a young man he was a dandy who sometimes

overdressed with an appalling (and provincial) bad taste
did not tell against him: most of his countrymen would
have liked to own his well-publicized wardrobe (though
irreverent little boys, seeing him in his carefully chosen
white riding-habit on his white horse, would ask him if
he were posing for his monument). His elopement with
a duchess, his later appropriation of another man's wife,
and his well-publicized life as sexual *condottiere* generated even more fame and admiration among his fellow-
countrymen; he was, after all, living out the favourite
myth of the Italian male.

His fame grew steadily from the time he was first published until the end of the first decade of this century.
Mussolini himself, who was both fascinated and annoyed
by d'Annunzio's egocentricity, shrewdly accorded him official recognition by sponsoring and financing a monumental,
forty-nine-volume finely printed, deluxe edition of his *opera
omnia*. Ironically enough, even such an unusual honor
proved to be insufficient to enable the poet to keep a prominent place among his peers. D'Annunzio's star, which had
risen so fast and so high, began declining steadily in an ir-
reversible motion which neither the sympathy of the Fascist
regime nor that of the faithful coterie of his critics-admirers
could change. As he approached his death in 1938, he found
himself almost forgotten, although still imitated, passé, as
it were, in an era that both believed and practised the very
cult of superman he had done so much to create.

His death, however, did not stop the growth of the in-
dustry of scholarship. The number of books, essays, notes,
and marginalia about d'Annunzio is large enough to stagger
the imagination. An entire yearly review, *Quaderni Dan-
nunziani*, is exclusively devoted to his work; over one hundred and ten books dealing directly or laterally with d'Annunzio and hundreds of serious articles about him have
appeared since his death, making him, along with Dante
and Manzoni, one of the most discussed authors of Italian
literature. What were the factors that contributed to his
meteoric rise in the literary firmament of his country? Even

a cursory examination of his extraordinary life yields ample evidence of the elements of his personal and cultural magnetism.

D'Annunzio was born in Pescara on March 12, 1863. As a young boy, he was enrolled in the Royal Boarding School Cicognini. Of his early experiences, perhaps the most memorable is his encounter with the poetry of Giosue Carducci. On his way back to the school in 1878, he purchased a copy of Cardducci's *Odi barbare,* a book that had a tremendous impact upon his sensibility. The youngster, whose penchant for poetry was becoming clearer every day, was much impressed by the work's robust, classical, and vibrant style. The opportunity to demonstrate tangibly how Carducci had affected him came when it was rumored that King Umberto I might stop to visit the Collegio: since his birthday fell on March 14, young Gabriele decided that it would be as fitting an occasion as any for a poem written in his Majesty's honor. The king did not visit the school, but the poem his admirer had composed did not fail to impress both his teachers and his family. Indeed, Don Francesco was so dazzled by his son's genius that he decided, somewhat against Gabriele's wishes, to publish his compositions at his own expense. The volume, titled *Primo vere,* appeared in 1879 under the pseudonym "Floro" with a dedication that says much about the young author: "*Mihi, Musis et paucis amicis,*" ("For me, for the Muses and for a few friends"). It is particularly puzzling to understand what exactly d'Annunzio had in mind when he wrote "few friends," since he managed to dispose rather quickly the five hundred copies of that first edition of his work. The sensuality of the lyrics in his volume perturbed many of its readers, as well as the school's principal, Flaminio del Seppia, who feared the adverse publicity it would bring to the school, therefore damaging a reputation he had worked so hard to achieve. Fortunately, no disciplinary action was taken against Gabriele, and "Floro" soon became known and admired by the literary critics as a promising poet, certainly one of the best of the younger generation, an opinion supported by the publication of a new, enlarged edition of *Primo vere.*

In 1881, after graduating with the highest honors, d'Annunzio enrolled at the University of Rome and went to work for a lively and controversial humorous paper, *Capitan Fracassa*, edited by Edoardo Scarfoglio, husband of the well-known novelist Matilde Serao. D'Annunzio's reputation continued to grow steadily, and the publication in 1882 of *Canto novo* [new song], a volume brought out by the influential editor of *Cronaca Bizantina*, Angelo Sommaruga, proved again that the critics' expectations had been amply justified. That same year, d'Annunzio published another volume of poems, *Terra vergine* [Virgin soil]; in 1883, more poems collected in *Intermezzo di rime*, whose sensuality was the cause of strident polemics. There followed *Il libro delle vergini* (a work whose contents brought the young author and his publisher to a confrontation that resulted in their parting ways after a mutually profitable association), *San Pantaleone*—both books collections of short stories that were to appear in a single volume with the title *Le novelle della Pescara* (1886; *Tales of my Native Town*, N.Y., 1920). From 1886 on, until shortly before the outbreak of World War I, hardly a year passed by without some of his books appearing. Between 1891 and 1900 d'Annunzio had completed most of his fiction, including *Il piacere* (1889; *The Child of Pleasure*, N.Y., 1896), *Giovanni Episcopo* (1891; *Episcopo & Co.*, Chicago, 1896), *L'innocente* (1892; *The Intruder*, N.Y., 1919), *Il trionfo della morte* (1894; *The Triumph of Death*, N.Y., 1896), *Le vergini delle rocce* (1895; *The Maidens of the Rocks*, N.Y., 1925), and *Il fuoco* (1900; *The Flame*, N.Y., 1906).

Poetry, his first love, and plays both in verse and prose were genres seldom neglected by the author. After his *Intermezzo di rime* [Intermezzo of poems] (1883), there followed *Elegie romane* [Roman elegies] (1887), *L'Isottèo* (1886), *La Chimera* (1888), *Il poema paradisiaco* [The heavenly poem] (1891), and *Alcyone* (1903)—the last two to this day choice d'Annunzio—*La città morta* (1898; *The Dead City*, Chicago, 1911), *La Gioconda* (1898; *La Gioconda*, N.Y., 1915), *Francesca da Rimini* (1902; *Francesca da Rimini*, N.Y., 1933), *La figlia di Jorio* (1904; *The Daughter of Jorio*, Boston, 1907), and *La nave* (1908; *La nave*, N.Y., 1909) are but a handful of the numerous plays and "mysteries" penned by the prolific d'Annunzio.

The fast pace of his literary activity did not prevent the poet from living a personal life that was in every sense equally hectic and intense. After a number of youthful but robust romances, d'Annunzio fell in love with Maria Hardouin di Gallese, whose family was one of the pillars of Roman aristocracy. The two eloped to Florence, and on July 28, 1883 the official religious ceremony was finally performed, even though it could hardly be said that the union was blessed by the bride's family (many of whom failed to show up for the ceremony), nor for that matter d'Annunzio's, singularly absent on that most important of occasions. About the only things that can be said for that marriage is that it brought some happiness for a few years and produced three children, Mario, Gabriellino, and Veniero, born respectively in 1884, 1886, and 1887. The truth is that d'Annunzio was simply unable to be content with a normal relationship. His liason with a Sicilian princess, Maria Gravina Cuyllas di Ramacca produced two more children, a daughter named Renata in 1893 and Gabriele Dante in 1897. In 1895, d'Annunzio had an affair with Eleonora Duse, who was to inspire a number of works, particularly plays. Here again, Gabriele was to demonstrate his shifting allegiance by promising a play for his mistress but actually writing it for Duse's archrival, Sarah Bernhardt.

Aside from his literary activities before the outbreak of World War I, d'Annunzio became also involved with politics. In 1897 he ran for and won a seat in the House of Representatives, a post he lost a few years later when his constituency decided that someone else, better trained and more understanding of the demands of public office, should be elected. Interwoven with his artistic pursuits were more extramarital affairs: with a Signorina X, with Barbara Leoni, Alessandra Cardlotta di Ruini, Nathalie de Goloubeff, to name just a few women who entered his life. Their names would be forgotten were it not for the role they played: d'Annunzio turned to them for much of his inspiration, to be sure. But he also extracted from them the kind of material of human experience he was to use so convincingly and astutely in his work.

If there was another element that characterizes his life, it surely must be the constant harrassment to which he was subjected by his creditors throughout most of life. Often, his movements are those of an adventurous and resourceful man unable to lead a less ostentatious life and thus forced to charge his purchases and bills to the accounts of his friends, family, and publishers. In 1910 the situation became so critical that the poet left for Paris, where he enjoyed much esteem.

His literary creativity continued unabated. In 1910 he published *Forse che sí forse che no* [Perhaps yes, perhaps not], one of the first long narratives about flying, a skill d'Annunzio mastered in his usual inimitable way. One of his most extraordinary successes was *Le martyre de Saint Sébastien*, a play set to music. The fact that the Vatican, in a 1911 decree, had placed all of d'Annunzio's work on the *Index Librorum Prohibitorum* [Index of forbidden books] certainly contributed to his ever-increasing popularity. Together with *Le martyre*, still another work, *La Pisanelle, ou la Mort Parfumé*—set to music by Pietro Mascagni —earned him the admiration of the French intellectual community. D'Annunzio's *Le Chèvrefeuille* (1914; *The Honey-suckle*, N.Y., 1916) was performed in Russia and South America, and *Francesca da Rimini* (set to music by Riccardo Zandonai) also received excellent notices.

The outbreak of World War I and the serious damages inflicted upon French art by the German troops aroused the poet's indignation. He returned to Italy on May 15, 1915 and began a series of appearances and effective speeches urging his countrymen to put pressure on the government to step into the conflict on the side of France and England. When war was declared, d'Annunzio volunteered and served in all three branches of the military. Among his many daring missions are the so-called *Beffa di Buccari* (the 1918 raid in the Trieste harbour that succeeded in inflicting severe damages to several large Austrian battleships) and his flights over Pola and Vienna, where he dropped propaganda leaflets. Such boldness and rare courage carried a price, and the poet was wounded several times and lost one eye. He was promoted regularly because of his bravery, and his distinguished service won him several decorations by the Italian and English governments.

D'Annunzio had entertained the idea that Italy's claims, colonial or otherwise, would be honored at the end of the war. The Treaty of Versailles, which managed to bypass practically every demand Italy made, was a great disappointment for the poet, whose frustration and anger found an outlet in his ambitious plans for Fiume and Zara on the Dalmatian coast. In 1919, at the head of a small group of faithful legionnaires, he occupied the city of Fiume and named himself commander. The national government, however, had different ideas about the question of border territories. The following year Italy and Jugoslavia signed a pact concerning the future status of Fiume, making d'Annunzio's position untenable both from the practical and political point of view. Efforts were made to persuade him of the futility of his position—to no avail. Only force, or the threat of force, could and did make clear that the last act of that play was about to begin. Weeks of negotiations produced no tangible results: troops were sent in and, in the ensuing clash, several soldiers lost their lives.

On January 18, 1921, accompanied by Luisa Baccara, a Venetian pianist, the poet installed himself in a small villa on the lake of Garda. He was not to actively participate in the political events of the following crucial years. Although he sympathized with the aspirations, and probably the methods, of the Fascists and was one of their ideological forerunners, he withdrew from politics.

In 1924 King Victor Emanuel III, acceding to Mussolini's request, named d'Annunzio Prince of Montenevoso. His much-enlarged residence, now dutifully rebaptized *Il Vittoriale* was decreed a national monument. From the 1920s to his death by cerebral hemorrhage on March 1, 1938, d'Annunzio spent much of his time supervising the publication of his *Opera Omnia*, edited by Giovanni Mardesteig. He continued to write, sporadically and without the richness of inspiration and vein of former days. His *Cento e cento e cento e cento pagine del libro segreto di Gabriele d'Annunzio* contains many moving pages, ever so rich with autobiographical details that reveal to us a good deal about the poet. But, as Mario Praz lucidly remarks in his introductory essay to the Ricciardi edition of d'Annunzio's choice pages, he was already an "ancient" writer whose work would continue to be read for historical reasons even though they had lost the capacity to speak to a new generation of readers.

The biographical outline just offered, brief as it must be, cannot hope to do justice to a life which was in every respect unusually complicated and flamboyant. There are a couple of observations that should properly be made at this point: first, d'Annunzio's life was so extravagant and his position in matters of aesthetics, morality, and politics so extreme and, at least for his time so controversial, that it was and is still problematical for a literary historian to offer a reasonably unbiased view on d'Annunzio's creative work; second, so diversified was the man's genius, so numerous his interests, and so uneven his artistic performance, that an assessment of his creative writing is inevitably less than fair if reached through an analysis of only one of the genres he practised.

There is, in this paradoxical situation, at least one comforting side: the present generation of readers, brought up in a substantially less repressed awareness of sexuality, is no longer shocked by what at the turn of the century were considered to be obscene pages. Indeed, the emphasis on a more legitimate literary judgment requests that we focus our attention on more substantive questions: did d'Annunzio succeed in representing the decadence of his characters? How well was his sensuous view of life objectified by and through the plot of his novels and the actions of his heroes? What did the author contribute to changing a tradition he had inherited? To answer these fundamental questions, we may turn to *Il piacere*, the first novel d'Annunzio wrote, certainly his most representative, and probably his best.

The book tells a rather simple story. Andrea Sperelli of

Ugenta, a wealthy Roman aristocrat, a *bon vivant*, connoisseur of art and himself a gifted artist, has been left by his mistress, Elena Muti. After challenging a rival to a duel, he is seriously wounded and leaves for Schifanoja, the villa of a cousin, in order to recover. It is there that he meets a gracious, introspective young matron, Donna Maria Ferres who is the wife of the Ambassador of Guatemala. The two fall quickly in love, and Andrea is given to understand that some day Maria will physically reciprocate his love. Back in Rome, Andrea once again sees his former mistress and hopes that, despite the fact that she is now married to Lord Heathfield, a wealthy English aristocrat, she will consent to resuming their love affair. Things, however, do not work out quite this way. Andrea, still yearning for Elena, gradually comes to love her through Maria. When Maria's husband, having contracted a large gambling debt he is unable to pay, flees from Rome, she gladly gives herself to him — only to be horrified when during their love-making he cries out the name of his former mistress. The book closes with Maria departing from Rome and Andrea more lonely and wretched than ever.

So much, or enough, for the story itself. As for the atmosphere of the novel, that admittedly is something else. Seldom before (or for that matter since) has another writer managed to match d'Annunzio's re-creation of the incredibly pretentious, sophisticated, and bored life of the Roman aristocracy in the 1880s. We move amidst the "beautiful people" of post-*Risorgimento* Rome; we hear their conversations about futile matters — mistresses, *objets d'art* being auctioned, the latest gossip — and we are privileged to be present as invisible observers of the gaiety of their drawing rooms and the intimacy of their bedrooms. There is nothing wrong, to be sure, with the milieu or with the special focus of d'Annunzio: indeed, the social and moral decadence he portrays could have been an immensely fascinating matter in other hands. The problem is not with the subject itself, but with the way the subject is treated. There is little, if indeed any irony in the book, and by and large (the single exception being toward the end of the novel) d'Annunzio is satisfied with skimming the surface, of giving us the picture but not its true flavor, concentrating on the colors and shapes of the things that constitute the milieu but not the essence of the souls that inhabit it.

This manner of treating a serious subject ends by being extremely damaging to it. Andrea Sperelli is nothing more than an effete intellectual, a sensitive but basically hollow aesthete who in some ways resembles Machiavelli's prince. Like the prince, Andrea is unreal, a figure with no depth, constructed for the sole purpose of illustrating the novelist's intention of giving form to the abstract ideal of a man seeking to make pleasure both a means and an end. To be sure, we do hear a good deal about various kinds of pleasures. Yet, the superlatives and refined language used to define such pleasure not once give us much of an insight into the experiences being described. Likewise, there is in the book a complacent, almost studious overindulgence in describing the "things," the physical habitat of the characters—something that probably inspired Mario Praz to state flatly in his excellent introductory essay to the anthological Ricciardi edition of d'Annunzio's work: "If we really reflect about the impression d'Annunzio's novels make on us, we realize that what is positive [about them] comes not from [their] psychology, but from [their] atmosphere . . . we remember things, not people. As in Arcimboldi's paintings, we have nothing to do with men, but [only] with things. . . . Through atmosphere and things, d'Annunzio tries to create human beings: but as we draw closer to them we become aware of the stuff they are made of."

The problem of his art is directly traceable to a human flaw. As d'Annunzio's distinguished English biographer Frances Winwar remarks: "Essentially his genius lay in the acuity of those senses, to which he had given full play. He delighted in the things he saw, the emotions he felt, the music he adored and desired as through an extension of his eroticism. Yet the very force of his sensations dulled him to a human appreciation of the feelings of others." All throughout the novel, the author strives to present the intellectual side of Andrea: aside from being knowledgeable in matters of art, he collects precious bric-a-brac and old furniture; he is a fine drawing artist and a gifted engraver; he delights in being able to discern the refined from the good with a sure, practical awareness of the monetary value of the things he purchases or admires. In addition, he is intimately acquainted with the classics, which he cites frequently: he is also at home in several European literatures and quotes liberally from Goethe, Byron, Shelley, Swinburne, and others. Music is another of his interests, and he is well versed in the works of Bach, Beethoven, Chopin, Schumann, Haydn, Mozart, Boccherini, and Cherubini, as well as the lesser-known Paisiello and Rameau. Finally, Andrea's encyclopediac knowledge extends to modern languages, particularly French, Spanish, and English, freely sprinkled throughout the book. Andrea is presented as an exceedingly well-informed gentleman, to be sure; but his knowledge, his intellectual equipment play no significant role in the development of his character. In the final analysis, culture appears as something merely superimposed on the persona of the story, to the point of existing for its own sake. Love itself is treated with the only dimension of libidinous appetite, as an insatiable appetite that reduces Andrea to a kind of sexual maniac so engrossed in sexuality that life passes him by without making much more than fleeting impressions upon him.

The Child of Pleasure is also a hopelessly romantic novel, romantic in the worst possible meaning of the term, both with respect to its theme and its style. Human relations are noted but never analyzed: thus, for example, Andrea's first mistress, Elena, breaks her affair with him for reasons that, since never explained, are for the reader to imagine. On the scant evidence offered by the novelist, we are to believe that Elena, however deep her love for Andrea may have been, decides to leave him on the grounds that her financial situation is so critical that she must marry a man of great means, Lord Heathfield, in order to continue living in the style to which she has become accustomed. After she has broken off with Andrea, she consents to visit him in their old love nest, Palazzo Zuccoli, where Andrea resides, for reasons that are never made clear since she gives no evidence of wanting to resume their liason. If we turn to Donna Maria, Andrea's second great love, we are no less baffled. Here is a woman of grace and sensitivity who, wretchedly married to a diplomat, falls in love with the hero of the novel in a matter of a few days, although it takes her considerably more time to bring herself to the physical consummation of her love. She does so, however, only when her husband is forced to depart in a hurry when he is unable to repay his gambling debts. Love itself, so fervently cherished in all of d'Annunzio's books, is pervasively thought of in incestuous terms (the highest form of love is described as a love between brother and sister), while, when consummated, it has the connotations of a religious experience (the bed is called "the altar"). Finally, there are the usual stock items of the romantic novel: aside from a sentimental kind of love, there is a duel, a serious wound, passionate love affairs, and a language that, at the crucially dramatic points, degenerates in clichés: "Adieu!" "Farewell!" "Love me forever!" While these sound like, and may even be touching words when properly and sparingly used, they lose their tension and impact by being overstressed in d'Annunzio's work and confuse the reader in his effort to gain significant insights into what such "love" is about. Can love be nothing more than a masochistic or sadistic experience, a form of punishment inflicted upon another human being—an experience utterly devoid of any uplifting elements? "Each of these loves," comments d'Annunzio apropos of Andrea, "brought him to a new degradation; each inebriated him with evil rapture, without satisfying him; each taught him some special subtlety of vice yet unknown to him. He had in him the seeds of all infections. He corrupted and was corrupted." In a letter addressed to his friend Francesco Paolo Michetti, which serves as a preface to the novel, d'Annunzio claims that his work was essentially a study of corruption, depravity, and of "many other subtleties and falsities and vain cruelties." By focusing on Andrea's existence, the author's intention was to condemn, if only by implication, a decadent life-style that poisons the human character. What ultimately dissatisfies the reader is not the theme of the book but d'Annunzio's conception of how his theme is to be artistically realized. His constant "denunciation" of the debauchery of his hero is inconclusive and unconvincng because it is stated, discussed, but never really depicted in any depth. In short, the reader is asked to accept without seeing the degradation of Andrea Sperelli. To achieve his objective, d'Annunzio uses a technique based heavily on an inordinate accumulation of details of a merely external kind. The problem raised by such a technique must be seen from the larger perspective of just what it contributes, or fails to contribute, to the work as a whole. Here one can hardly take issue with Moravia's opinion that the obsession with objects is indicative of d'Annunzio's intention of "affixing a maximum attention and immobility to every detail as if it stood by itself and had no connection with what comes before and follows after. . . . Page follows page composed not structurally, but according to purely extrinsic demands."

No one, I suspect, would claim that *The Child of Pleasure* is a great, or even a good novel. By the same token, it can hardly be dismissed for it does reflect a break with the traditions of *verismo* and the historical novel. It is, in a very special way, a personal novel in which reality and imagination are fused in such a way that literature is transformed from the mirror of life into a "way of life." When pressed on this issue, d'Annunzio could affirm, as he actually did in discussing his work *The Triumph of Death* with the French writer Romain Rolland, "[My book] is in no sense a work of the imagination but a representation of life." Yet, when his mistress Barbara Leoni came upon the notes d'Annunzio had been writing about their love affair, the poet insisted, without batting an eyelash, that there was "no connection between reality and a work of art."

D'Annunzio was not only a writer but, as noted earlier, something of an ideologist who regarded his literary work, as well as his individual actions, as proper vehicles to define within their respective limitations his concepts of man and society. A closer look at Andrea Sperelli reveals that, much like the majority of Dannunzian characters, he embodies the qualities of Nietsche's *Uebermensch*, the superman. The *Uebermensch* follows a cult of superiority achieved through cultural, racial, or physical strength, or any combination of these and other expressions of the self. Similarly, the artist is assigned to a privileged position in society, set on a pedestal apart from the others, clearly contemptuous of the masses and any democratic political system of government. Military and political power has an important role to play in the world of superman, since presumably it alone can restore the former prestige and glory of the *patria*. Such nationalism of the most parochial sort is accompanied by a cheap, vulgar brand of patriotism (of the lurid kind we have seen lately in our own political wasteland) which stresses achievement of objectives through any means, usually violent, blood baths and complete elimination of those who, unable to share aspirations similar to ours, must be considered cowards, uninformed, naïve, and expendable.

If *Il piacere* foreshadows the figure of superman, *L'innocente* (*The Intruder*) d'Annunzio's third novel, brings *Uebermensch* to its fuller realization. Tullio Hermil is in love with his wife Giuliana, of whom he demands an absolute fidelity he himself does not feel obliged to return. In a moment of weakness, Giuliana has an affair with a novelist, Filippo Arborio. Upon learning that she will have a child, she and her husband, who knows of the extramarital relation, begin making plans to kill the offspring—a murder they eventually carry out by exposing the baby to the rigors of the weather. Theirs is a crime, but there will not be a punishment. As Tullio declares, at the beginning of what is essentially a confession-type novel, "I have committed a crime. . . . Man's justice does not touch me. No earthly court could ever judge me."

It is instructive to turn to d'Annunzio's fourth novel to perceive just how the superficial intellectualism that characterizes *The Child of Pleasure* evolves into a novel with regional, mystical, and anthropological excesses: *Il trionfo della morte* (*The Triumph of Death*). Less pretentious than d'Annunzio's earlier novels, *The Triumph of Death* is particularly rewarding in terms of its vivid sense of the primitive, hard existence in the Abruzzi region. Sections of the book, particularly those depicting the extreme poverty, superstitions, and abysmal number of illnesses afflicting the peasantry, surely rank among d'Annunzio's best pages. Once again the book's central theme is the love of Giorgio Aurispa for a married woman, Ippolita Sanzio, whose human flaw is her inability to conceive a child. Theirs is a highly sensual love, always striving to achieve a perfection possible only when Ippolita completely surrenders herself —her body and mind—to her lover. Her mission becomes that of catering to and satisfying the libido of her mate to the point that she changes into a kind of lustful animal, while Giorgio's own sensuality becomes intellectualized through his monologues and broodings. Unlike Andrea Sperelli's passion, which is mundane and refined, Giorgio's is savage and destructive. When he realizes that Ippolita's lust can no longer be satisfied, he concludes that he is no more a free man, freedom being equated to sexual superiority. He sees himself doomed to becoming slave to the woman he had sought to master, and realizes that such threat must ultimately be stopped by violence. One day, as he tries to push Ippolita down a precipice, he becomes locked in a brutish embrace. The couple plunge down to death and to a final liberation from an unbearable existence.

Despite its dramatic moments and its occasional suspense, the novel is not an exciting, profound work, nor does it contribute much to a clarification and elaboration of its author's vision of the world. On the other hand, the novel shows an effort to move away from the standard treatment of a story. As reflected in their individual titles, the six parts of the work serve a dual purpose: to carry out the plot to its inevitable denouement and to give us some insights into the circumstances that went into the making of the character of the hero, for example, chapter two, "La casa paterna." The broader strategy of d'Annunzio is to develop and bring to fruition the theme of the protagonist's tendency toward murder and suicide, intimated at the beginning of the book.

Such brief synopses as I have given of d'Annunzio's novels give only a notion of the kind of world he depicted time and again in his narratives. A careful reading of his novels bring out what are their essential characteristics. Their beauty and effectiveness is at best sporadic, limited to a few pages, especially when they are descriptive. Only then does the poet's real genius emerge in full evidence: his formidable sensitivity (perhaps unmatched by any poet in Italian letters except Petrarch) of the musicality of words; his capacity to create subtle, if short-lived effects through the use of archaic, refined, or invented words; his occasional ability to suggest the temperament of his characters through the descriptions of their milieu. There is also evidence, however, that d'Annunzio, for all his eagerness to be at once the spectator, the reporter, the painter, *and* the judge of the decadent society of his tales, became himself caught in the web of the world he sought to portray. Even insofar as his expressive instrument is concerned, as Giuseppe Petronio points out in his monographic essay on the poet, "it is impossible to distinguish. . . . nature from fiction, honesty from falsehood, so closely and inextricably are they woven together." Hailed for the elegance of his style, to the modern reader d'Annunzio sounds artificial and precious: and while his stylistic resources and resourcefulness retain some of their magnetism, they are hardly sufficient to maintain our curiosity in his writings. His vision of life is seldom convincing and even more seldom profound: on the contrary, the textual evidence points to the fact that the world d'Annunzio saw and claimed to be true was the product of a fervid imagination and a distorted mind. His plots are farfetched, artificial, and contrived; his characters have little human and psychological depth and are rarely convincing as human beings. A master plagiarist, d'Annunzio borrowed freely from the works of classical antiquity as well as from the works of his own era and earlier periods. Perhaps he may ultimately be recognized as a superb technician of words rather than an "engineer of the soul"—Quasimodo's description of a true poet. He used language as an end in itself rather than an instrument to give form to his view of life. Never a visionary, he lacked the ideals, the artistic discipline, and the sense of purpose of a true artist, and he is thus remembered primarily for the way he wrote rather than *what* he wrote. The crowning irony of d'Annunzio's life is that, despite his exceptional bravery on the battlefield and his unusual sensitivity to the expressive values of art, he left his nation a legacy of words, not symbols; of conceits, not ideas; of images, not ideals.

Women Writers: Neera and Aleramo

Writing in the twenties, the critic Giuseppe Ravegnani posed this question:

> Is there, in Italy, a feminine literature in the traditional sense, that is to say, something lively, well-nourished, spontaneous, that has definite and clear ties with our own literate climates? Or [is there] at least an exceptional temperament, an intellectual shrew, a woman-monster? Now, there are some [women] writers, five or six excellent [at that]: but we do not believe there is a real and well-defined feminine literature. What such literature there is, by and large lives and nourishes itself on the margins of another greater, greatly more sober and conclusive [literature]. It seems to us. . . . that feminine literature, particularly the recent one, has the habit of putting on trousers, and has the mania of putting on its face an unprejudiced and even cynic mask. Now, there are no worse misfortunes than a bad copy of a literature that is already dislikeable and even fruitless among men writers. . . . As for us, we would like a woman, particularly if prolific, to be old-fashioned, maybe romantic, homey, and a little exhausted by housework; that is to say, concerned with what can well be a world precluded to man's observation, frightened to misrepresent and offend the intimate secret of femininity.

As is frequently the case when controversial questions are discussed, Ravegnani missed the opportunity of coming to grips with a generally slighted issue which turned out to be more important than it was believed. In the present case, the critic failed to recognize the handwriting on the wall. Socioeconomic changes, such as those undergone by Italy after the unification, invariably hasten the liberalization of certain traditions and bring about new values. One of the most central novelties of the cultural scene in Italy was the emergence of a growing number of women writers who found an audience prepared and eager to read what they had to say. That Ravegnani should assume a stance pretty much in harmony with prevailing attitudes deeply rooted in the mores of his country can hardly come as a surprise to us. After all, even if, as Olga Ragusa claims in her essay "Women Novelists in Postwar Italy," "the tradition of the learned woman, indeed, of the artist woman, reaches far back into Italian history," it is also true that the women who made their mark in literature in Italy had been, up to the nineteenth century, very few and generally of no great consequence in terms of their influence. Now the situation began to change as the role of women became more important as they began, at first modestly, to play more than just a passive role in Italian life. It is a sad but historically indisputable fact that until the early part of this century Italy lacked a strong feminine literature, that is to say, a literature written by, about, but not exclusively for an audience of women, reflecting to some degree a woman's point of view or ideology. This state of affairs is not peculiarly Italian, but is typical of certain Latin countries (Spain and Portugal) and Latin American nations, where there has seldom been much sympathy for women with intellectual and creative interests. In the social order of such countries the woman occupies a place with well-defined functions: she gives birth to children, she assists her husband in his occupation or business, in his social or political pursuits, content with playing ancillary roles even when she manages to have something to say about how the family's affairs should be run. For all the influence she may have, however, her status has been and continues to be, though in a lesser way, somewhat unclear and ill-defined.

The emergence of a feminine literature in Italy is not only an intriguing occurrence per se, but one of the significant events of the whole post-*Risorgimento* cultural history. For a variety of reasons, Italy lagged well behind her sister nation France with respect to the question of the involvement of women in the critical and creative process. The social standing of the women was, as it has been hinted, not a very envious one. Of course, Italy did have her share of *salons*, where men and women of a certain social and intellectual standing met to discuss the significant literary events, books, and personalities of the day. The trend intensified with the passing of time, even though the *salons* and the brilliancy of their participants could hardly match their French counterparts: Mme de Sévigné, Mme de la Fayette, Mme de Staël. There are other elements that delayed the coming of age of the woman artist, one of which was the inadequate education and intellectual training most women (except the few who could be privately tutored) received. Illiteracy, put at 75 percent in 1875, was another appalling reality that had to be confronted and corrected. The question of illiteracy is especially crucial if we bear in mind that since time immemorial women, not men, have constituted the largest segment of the reading audience.

The potentials of a readership made up largely of women was certainly not a nineteenth-century discovery. The great fourteenth-century master storyteller Giovanni Boccaccio publicly took notice of his prospective audience, when in the strategic introduction to his *Decameron* he modestly (and, one might add, astutely) stated that his work was addressed to "women with plenty of time on their hands." Ever since then, and particularly with the rise of a middle class keenly interested in education, writers have shown a special alertness to the question of who reads whom, what, and why—a problem frankly and repeatedly discussed. In 1793, in an article published in the *Guardian*, Joseph Addison remarked: "There are some reasons why learning is more adapted to the female world than the male. As in the first place, because they have more spare time on their hands, and lead a more sedentary life. . . . There is another reason why those especially who are women of quality, should apply themselves to the letters, namely, because their husbands are strangers to them." Indeed, as Ian Watt points out in his book *The Rise of the Novel*, since women in England (and, by extension, in other European countries as well) could not partake in many of the activities of their menfolk, they had a great deal of leisure which "was often occupied by their omniverous reading."

The changed political situation in Italy brought about vast social changes, of which the marked emancipation of the women in the closing decades of the century was probably one of the factors that heavily contributed to the emergence of a feminine literature. Perhaps the greatest revolution to take place in Italy was right inside of the home: "Up until the first half of the nineteenth century. . . . the family was conceived as a true and real community, which tended to grow always larger with the addition of new elements—marriages and births." Much of what life there was, particularly for the women, took place in the home. There was little, if any, activity outside of the home, and then what there was was strictly necessary to run the house: "shopping, paying or returning visits, attending weddings and other ceremonies." By all standards, it was a situation far from conducive to the healthy intellectual growth of a young woman.

After the middle of the nineteenth century, a greater loosening and liberalization of the whole structure of life inside and outside the home began taking place. Except in the *Mezzogiorno*, where ancient social traditions resisted the changes brought about by the new conditions, women began enjoying greater freedom of movement, of action, and of thought. They could now visit their friends without the customary formality and often unescorted could attend benefit events and frequent the theatres. In short, as Ottavio Barié notes, "the political events that revolutionized Italy between 1848 and the Unification and beyond had a strong impact on family life, at times decisively changing its concept and customs. The most important fact was the disappearance of that ideal of patriarchical type that up until that time had prevailed almost everywhere: principal cause for this were the political events of the *Risorgimento*, and the reflection they had on social and private life. . . . The women, above all, felt the effect of the changed mentality and began venturing beyond the threshold of the home to participate in the aspirations and common ideas, perhaps to make her own contribution to the cause of Italy."

Reading books and discussing them became gradually part of the daily life of many a middle-class home. The proliferation and availability of newspapers and magazines contributed significantly, just as the radio and television were to do in later years, to the gradual improvement of the education of the populace, particularly with respect to the spread of a national language. The greater diffusion of books and the relative ease with which a private library, however small, could be put together were also of immense importance in that this created a readily available source of knowledge inside the home itself. As the reading public grew numerically and qualitatively, so did the awareness that an important segment of it, the women, longed to be addressed by other women intimately acquainted with the special problems and outlook of their sex. The sexual revolution was budding slowly but surely. Now gradually released from the drudgery of housework, women began to look at themselves, probing deeply in their mind as to what they really were, and discovered that as human beings they too were entitled to think and articulate their emotions as men had done and would continue to do. The word for such an awareness was *feminism*, and its goal was not so much the attainment of parity with men in every area—a target most women realistically knew to be unattainable without a prolonged struggle—but the achievement of sufficient emancipation to enable women to fulfill a measure of their potentials in the field of their choosing.

That women gradually made their points is evidenced by the fact that publishers began responding to the new mood, since they could hardly ignore it intellectually, and from a purely business point of view it would have been unsound not to exploit the opportunities it offered. Because the price of books was frequently above the reach of a housewife, the works of many writers, men and women alike, appeared in serialized form in the newspapers and reviews, following a custom that had proved its worth in several European countries, particularly France and England.

The two women novelists of the period under consideration reached prominence almost at once; in some cases, interest in what they wrote has already survived the first crucial test of time. Beside their individual artistic merits, what matters about them is they produced work of a significantly high level which assured that in the future women of literary talent would no longer be excluded from the cultural scene. The novelists chosen are, of course, quite different from one another: yet, they both eschew parochial interests in feminine problems, even though they write with special insight about the world as lived and as seen by women. Knowingly or not, they helped bring about a new awareness of the woman and her relation to the "other" world of men. After their entrance in the cultural mainstream and the attention they attracted by men and other women alike, life would no longer be the same.

Neera: The Pathos of the Woman

Among women writers in Italy, Neera (nom de plume of Anna Radius Zuccari) is probably the most conservative and, at the same time, is both generous and understanding of a woman's lot. Throughout her long creative life Neera concentrated on what is basically a single theme: the inadequate, unrealistic upbringing a woman receives as she prepares herself to assume the burdensome responsibilities of a wife and a mother. "The woman nowadays is neither respected nor loved as she should be; her name is everywhere; her image lavishly used in advertisements on every wall," wrote Neera in one of her essays. If her protest sounds quite timely it is because she was among the first novelists in her country to take notice of how a woman was being exploited by being reduced to a mother and a sex symbol at the expense of her humanity. There is some evidence that suggests that Neera did not stumble into this realization accidentally. She had personally experienced the wonderful expectations of every young girl, she had entertained her share of illusions, and she ultimately understood the grief and torments of bad marriages by closely observing her own parents. She was born into a modestly comfortable middle-class family in Milan on May 7, 1846. She led a fairly quiet, if not altogether happy existence, whose major event was the loss of both her mother and father early in her life. Both parents had been quite aloof from her, and she found herself, as she was to write, "physically leading the existence of an old, dear lady." Because she had experienced much loneliness, she preferred as a writer analysis instead of flights of fancy, dealing with everyday reality rather than imaginary tales: the figure of her father and mother remain almost always in the background, as the center of the stage is occupied by "young girls transformed into fashionable puppets or heartless flirts by the frivolities of society. . . . noble hearts rising heroic through agonies of unspoken grief."

If this sketchy characterization seems too pessimistic, the impression must be corrected. Neera was married, apparently happily, to Adolfo Radius, lived a creative existence that won her distinction in her chosen field, and enjoyed the friendship and esteem of the outstanding men of her time, Luigi Capuana and Benedetto Croce among them. Though her private life could be labeled conventional, her creative career revealed rare zest, if we are to judge by the number of volumes of short stories, poetry, novels, essays of the moral and pedagogical type she wrote, an activity capped by the surprisingly and enormously successful popular book entitled *Dictionary of Hygiene for Family Use.*

The bulk of her literary output reflects her views on life from a feminine perspective, to be sure, but as Aldo Borlenghi stressed, also from the vantage point of a serious writer who visualized fiction as a vehicle to analyze rather than romanticize the fundamental problems of life as she saw them.

A warm endorsement by Benedetto Croce written in

1904, just fourteen years before her death (in 1918), was certainly responsible for the esteem Neera continued to enjoy for a good part of this century. What Croce admired most in her was not so much her gifts as an artist but her "solid and well-defined moral philosophy," her commitment to search for certain basic verities of life, and, last but not least, her courageous stance vis-à-vis the role of the woman in modern society. "They say," Neera herself wrote, "that the woman is considered a child-making machine. By the same token, one could also say that the sun is a heat-making machine, and one would be telling the truth; [but] it would be no less true because of this [to add] that the sun is the first and most poetic force in the universe." This is quite a revealing statement indeed in that it offers a metaphor that controls a great deal of her novels: the example of the sun, with its central position in the universe and its beneficial *raison d'être* is, after all, what Neera tries to come to grips with again and again. Just like the sun ("a heat-making machine," as well as "the first and most poetical force in the universe"), the woman commands by her biological structure a special role in life: she gives life to new lives and warmth to mankind, thus satisfying man's need to reproduce and a human need of love. But this is a little too abstract for Neera, who likes to deal concretely and practically with the role of a woman, particularly when social conditions are such that she is forced to endure far too much anguish and loneliness. Strangely, there are contradictions between the critical and the creative work of Neera. While in the former she expresses many reservations about the progress made by women in their struggle to gain certain unassailable rights, in her fiction the woman is presented as a being shackled by social conventions and prejudices, as a person whose upbringing has been such that she cannot feel free and capable of fulfilling herself as an individual. On the contrary, she must frequently accept the role of the mother-and-wife created for her by tradition. This is a point that receives particular attention in Neera's essays: it may not be always too unreasonable for society to think of a woman in terms of a stereotyped image, but it is unjust that she should be denied the opportunity of not marrying and still leading a life of dignity and purpose. And what about those women who, because of one reason or another, are spinsters? Neera wrote with great compassion about them, their suffering in being the objects of ridicule because of their irregular life pattern, "their relative, personal wretchedness, stifled in the vast sea of human miseries, neglected like a toothache is neglected by those with healthy teeth, is a wretchedness all the same. . . . This, after all, is the great injustice: society that deprives women of their natural rights whenever they have been unable to find a husband, makes fun of them if they remain spinsters, calling them mean, envious, sensual." Here as elsewhere Neera's writings are distinguished by a profound compassion for the outcasts, as well as a feeling of righteous indignation when men choose to disregard even the basic rights of a woman.

To see just how Neera's woman is portrayed, we may turn to her first novel, published in 1886, whose title is the name of the heroine. Teresa is a sweet, obedient, lovely child. Her mother is a rather passive person, her father, Signor Caccia, is a typical bourgeois: a strict guardian of family mores, authoritarian, selfish, and narrow-minded. As a good bourgeois, he also respects certain values: in the present case, he decides that given his limited income, no money will be set aside for Teresa's dowry. His first and only concern is with the future of his only son who, in due time (according to an old tradition) will be responsible for supporting his aging parents. Teresa falls in love with a young law student, Egidio Orlandi, who asks Signor Caccia for his daughter's hand in marriage and expresses the hope that he will help him financially to start a law practice. Egidio is not only turned down, but literally told he is never to set foot in the house again.

The opposition of Teresa's parents does not prevent the two young people from seeing each other whenever the opportunity arises. Egidio finishes his studies, works for a while in a law firm and then turns to journalism. As time goes by, the two see each other less and less. Meanwhile, Teresa's mother, whose health has never been very good, dies; one of Teresa's younger sisters marries, while her twin wins a competition for a teaching post in another town. Teresa's brother completes his university work and moves to another town; Signor Caccia suffers a stroke that dooms him to a wheelchair and soon enough passes away. Shortly after his death, Teresa receives an urgent plea from Egidio, who is very ill in nearby Parma and needs her help. Unafraid of the repercussions her action will have in town, Teresa leaves her home to be with the man she has so deeply and platonically loved for so many years.

The flaws of a social system that so freely sacrifices the life of a human being in the name of preposterous customs are obvious. What is unusual is Neera's ability to present the shocking situation dramatically, without any sermonizing or theorizing. The author withholds comments for the facts must, and do indeed, speak for themselves. Teresa's love for a decent young man is mercilessly prevented from budding without any valid justification. Ironically enough, the events of the story show how unnecessary, irrational, and cruel Signor Caccia's decision proves to be, since neither he nor his wife live to enjoy the kind of secure retirement for which they had sacrificed their daughter's happiness. The message is driven home quite persuasively: in a struggle between an individual and tradition, it is the former that must win out: and it is in this sense that Teresa's modest rebellion is not only perfectly understandable but justified as well.

Lydia, Neera's second novel, published in 1887, focuses on much the same milieu and characters. Lydia, the young protagonist, is an emancipated version of Teresa, and yet she too is ultimately defeated by the cruelties of life. Lydia is a very beautiful, much sought-after and considerably spoiled young lady. She lives with her widowed mother and her aging uncle Leopoldo. Lydia is always seen at the best parties, accompanied by the most handsome young men, and seemingly leading the life of a perennial debutante. One day, suddenly, her mother suffers a stroke that makes her totally dependent on others. Her illness exposes Lydia, for the first time in her life, to pain and the frailty of human existence. When her mother dies, Lydia's awareness of sufferings sharpens considerably. For a period of time she devotes herself to charitable work, but the brief interlude soon comes to an end, and she returns to her usual frenetic life and falls in love with an attractive army officer, Count Richard Kepsky. The two plan to marry, but an old friend, the lawyer Calmi, one of Lydia's undeclared admirers, tells her that Richard was dishonorably discharged from the army on account of having incurred some large gambling debts he is unable to repay. Moreover, Richard plans to marry her only to use her dowry to repay his debt. Finally, and this comes as a severe blow to Lydia, Richard is carrying on with one of Lydia's best friends, the Baroness Thea Von Stern. As a good friend, Calmi has tried to warn Lydia of the disaster that lies ahead if she goes through with her plans: at last, she confronts the truth of her situation. Coquettish, pretty, spoiled, but certainly not insensitive, well-meaning and even generous, Lydia finds herself a victim of her own weaknesses and her upbringing. Because she dreads the prospect of ending up as a spinster (a likely prospect now that her reputation has been seriously damaged by her affair with Richard), she decides to take her life and commits suicide using a small pistol purchased long ago precisely, although unconsciously, for such an occasion.

Both novels, written in a simple, restrained style, persuasively depict the condition of the woman as Neera sees it. She must conquer a male in order to occupy a place in the social world, a world that expects a great deal of her but holds but few promises; she is expected to become experienced in the difficult art of coquetry without losing her virginity, which would put her in the special category of outcasts. Finally, she contributes the largest share to her family while remaining exposed to a life fraught with pain and unhappiness.

Unquestionably, Neera's heart is in the right place, and she would qualify as a deliberately moderate liberal, at least in her fiction. The heroines of both novels reach the same fate by different paths—both ultimately doomed to an unhappy existence, or no existence at all, doomed to live out their lives by social conventions largely created by the men for their own benefit. The sufferings are clear, as are the repressive conditions that cause them in a woman. Yet, if one looks to Neera's essays for a more direct intellectual discussion of those situations so vividly presented in her fiction, one is bound to be severely disappointed. Thus, for example, while acknowledging that unfortunately some women cannot find a husband or do not feel fulfilled until they have children or channel their energies and intelligence to causes other than those traditionally prescribed—the home, the husband, children—she offers little alternative except to confess that, life being what it is, a woman must simply put up with the situation and resign herself to accept what has always been her role. Indeed, her essays and other writings reveal Neera's fears about the consequences of a woman's emancipation. The efforts to make a woman free, or at least freer than she has been, must be guided by caution and deliberation, lest they be counterproductive to the goal in mind. Indeed, at times her essays are replete with clichés of the worst sort: "A woman should remain in the place where she has done so much good for society. . . . The true slavery from which she must free herself is the materialistic concept of happiness . . ." Such comments scattered throughout her writings bring out the conservative and less persuasive side of her views, which may explain why today's readers prefer her novels and her short stories to her nonfiction for their capacity to dramatize how Neera felt, not what she merely thought, about human unhappiness and a woman's lot. We must bear in mind that her novels were written almost one century ago, and that they opened new ground by exploring with dignity and understanding the inferior position to which women were relegated. This by itself commends her to today's reader. Above and beyond that, as Luigi Russo perceptively noted, Neera "is perhaps the writer who has best felt and poetically translated the modesty of feminine passions." "Women," concluded Russo, "find in her a poetess who represents them with a shy intimacy of words and a nostalgic tenderness of feelings."

Sibilla Aleramo: The Woman as an Object

Among women writers in Italy and probably else-where, it would be difficult to find someone who led as stormy, unorthodox, and "liberated" existence as Sibilla Aleramo, the nom de plume of Rina Faccio. A prolific author, whose literary production includes lyrical poetry, autobiographical works, novels, a copious volume of cor-respondence with many leading artists of modern Italy, and a perceptive diary, Sibilla succeeded in spite of her numer-ous love affairs in retaining the respect and the affection of the readers and critics of a country where traditions die hard, if at all. She wrote in the same uninhibited way as she lived, without compromises, as a human being seeking to understand and to articulate something of the anguish and beauty of life as only a woman can experience it. She committed her deepest feelings to the printed page, never ashamed or hesitant to reveal her most private thoughts. She managed to accomplish this without offending public morality, for she never debased her work with vulgarities: somehow Aleramo kept her private life separate from her public life and asked that she be judged not on what she did, but on what she consigned to the readers as the distilla-tion in an artistic form of how she saw life.

Her books, controversial and shocking, found an im-mediate audience but not an equally receptive body of critics. Giuseppe Ravegnani, for example, expressed some reservations about Aleramo's sincerity, labeling it "docu-mentary and cruel." "In its effort to be and remain an ex-tremely lucid and precise mirror of the self that moves it," he continued, "it ends up reaching most of the time nega-tive meanings and results." Others reacted differently. Luigi Tonelli wrote that Aleramo "cannot be confused with any other [woman] writer. Not with [Grazia] Deledda, rough, masculine, powerful; not with [Matilde] Serao, cordially open to the spectacle of the outer world; not with [Ada] Negri, for whom love tends to become moral and spiritual, not with [Annie] Vivanti, a genius romantically unbridled and brilliant; not with [Amalia] Guglielminetti, exclusively sensual. . . . Sibilla is limited, but . . . singularly profound." Among those who had good words for her first novel was Luigi Pirandello: "Few modern novels I have read," he commented, "embrace such a serious and profound drama in its simplicity and represent it with equal art, in a form so noble and sincere, with an equal measure of control and power."

Sibilla Aleramo was born into a bourgeois family of Piedmontese stock on August 14, 1876, in the city of Alessandria, but was brought up in Milan. When her father was forced to take a managerial job in a glass factory in Porto Recanati in 1887, her formal education came to an abrupt end. Sibilla had managed to complete only the elementary grades. What education in the public schools never gave her because of circumstances, her readings of certain authors (Ibsen, Whitman, and Emerson among others) did. Like so many other writers, Sibilla was schooled by life itself: and life was anything but easy on her. Her mother, unable to accept a wretched marriage with a man she did not love, tried to commit suicide and became insane; her father, egocentric and insensitive, deserted his family; Sibilla herself, seduced when still a sixteen-year-old adolescent by a man in her father's employ, had to marry and live with the father of her child, a man she could neither respect nor love. Nine years later (now twenty-six) Sibilla broke away. She began writing for magazines (for a while she served as the editor of *L'Italia Femminile*), became friendly with many of her peers: Giovanni Cena, who discovered her and gave her the name Sibilla; Vincenzo Cardarelli, with whom she lived for two years; and the poet Dino Campana. "I acquired [then]," Sibilla notes in her *Diario*, "many of the attitudes that were to characterize [my personality]: I became a free lover, a writer, I imposed my rebellion and my boldness on society: and my own name changed to the present one."

Indeed, the various phases of her life were marked by her love affairs. The relations she had with many of the leading artists and intellectuals of her time proved to be far from incidental, peripheral escapades. On the contrary, they were events of great importance, chapters in her quest for self-knowledge, and as such they left their mark upon her sensibility. Her love affairs were, in a most serious way, encounters that enabled her to probe ever more deeply into the self, still other instruments of a quest based upon the conviction that, "a woman must find in herself her own vision of life and her own aesthetic laws," as she stated in yet another autobiographical book, *Andando e stando* [Going and staying] (1921). Every experience became a part of the human puzzle she attempted to put together that would ultimately provide some insights into the condition of herself as a woman.

In 1925, she was one of the few brave intellectuals to sign the anti-Fascist Manifesto drafted by the philosopher Benedetto Croce. Although for several years she did not actively oppose fascism (on the contrary, she wrote some mildly complimentary comments on the regime's achievements in the area of land reclamation in the north and south of Italy), she slowly moved toward a more radical political position. The outbreak of World War II proved to be the turning point: she joined the Communist party, became a militant supporter of its programs, spoke at numerous rallies of factory workers, read her poetry to her proletarian audiences. She died in Rome on January 13, 1960.

Una donna (A Woman at Bay, N.Y., 1908) has the distinction of being Sibilla Aleramo's first book, her first novel, and the most thoughtful and impressive narrative she wrote in her unusual artistic career. She was thirty years old when her novel was published in 1906. She had completed it two years earlier, eager to put her experience down on paper: the heroine-narrator of *Una donna* can hardly be taken for anyone else but the author herself. Autobiographical as the book undoubtedly is, it is grossly unfair to see it only as such, because what one may suspect to be personal events are transcended, allowing for that symbolic expansion without which no work of fiction can achieve universal significance. All this does not decrease the passion, the seriousness and sensitivity which enable a personal story to become a shocking document, a frank statement of the human itinerary of Sibilla Aleramo and, by extension, of women everywhere. We read the book and our initial impression is one of utter disbelief; yet its tone is so candid, the story so believable, that we cannot doubt either its sincerity or its truthfulness. The world we come to face is one in which women are regularly exploited or unmercifully sacrificed by men. This, in and by itself, is a sufficiently ugly and tragic reality. What makes it even more unbearable is that, given the situation which begins in the very early years of a woman's life, the relation between the two sexes begins on the wrong footing. So shoddy are the premises on which such a relationship is founded that they can only engender an ever-growing process of estrangement.

Questions, however, must still be asked, and answers be sought. Problems exist and they demand to be recognized and at least studied, if not resolved. And so Sibilla asks:

How can a man who has had a good mother become cruel toward the weak, disloyal toward a woman to whom he gives his love, a tyrant of his children? Yet a good mother must not be, as mine [was], a simple creature [to be] sacrificed: she must be a *woman*, a human being. But how can she become a woman if her family gives her, unaware, weak, incomplete [in marriage], to a man who does not receive her as an equal, uses her as a piece of property, gives her children [to bear] whom he abandons to her care, while he performs his social duties, so that he may continue to amuse himself as [he did when he was] a child?

The heroine of the story is a docile, good child: she loved her mother as a youngster, but her eyes were on her father, whom she worshipped: "Love for my father dominated [everything else]. I loved my mother, but I had an unlimited adoration for my father. . . . He was the luminous example to my small individuality, he who represented for me life's beauty."

All idealized pictures are bound to tarnish and soon enough the lofty, romantic image of her father begins to deteriorate. A science teacher at a local school, he quarrels with the principal and resigns from his post, accepting a partnership in the business of his brother-in-law living in Milan. The incident is the first of a series that contribute to a growing alienation of Sibilla from her family. At the age of eight, she begins to feel irritated by her mother's suggestion that she live less with her intellect and more with her feelings. No happy person herself, the mother attempts to take her own life by swallowing poison—an act that is the direct result of her growing depression. Other unhappy events follow, and Sibilla discovers purely by chance that her father has a mistress—an employee at the factory. "My father," she confesses, "the shining example, was changing all of the sudden into an object of horror. He, who had raised me with the cult of sincerity, loyalty, was hiding a side of his life from my mother, [and] from all of us." As it often happens at a crucial moment in the life of a growing girl, the discovery has the effect of dramatizing the evil, if indirect, consequences of sexual attraction. Soon afterward, Sibilla is exposed briefly to the manifestation of a sexual attraction that destroys her highly idealized and distorted concept of love: one day the young man who is courting her embraces her in a manner that seems to her brutish and demeaning. The unhappy home atmosphere further contributes to an uncertain, troubling revision of what the nature of love ought to be. And since the question is inadequately answered, it follows that happiness must be postponed to yet another stage of life. Where she had hoped that her period of courtship would be one filled with joy and delight, both are postponed until marriage with her suitor and then motherhood, with one disappointment following another. Attracted to another man, Sibilla is repelled by his sudden advances, yet, wishing to punish her husband she tells him that she has betrayed him. She then tries to take her life by swallowing poison, a destructive act patterned after her mother's. The attempt fails and Sibilla, in quest of the answer to her condition, turns to books, and in particular to the work of a sociologist who insists that a wife and a mother is also a woman—a realization that sparks the beginning of a new life for the heroine. She turns to writing, and her essays soon find their way into print. She is an immediate success and is offered a post with a magazine for women, a position she accepts as her husband is once again out of work. She moves to Rome and begins creating a new life for herself: life takes now a new dimension, and Sibilla realizes how wretched her past life has been, particularly in terms of the rights she was denied solely because of her sex.

One day her husband is asked to return to manage the factory in Milan from which he was dismissed. Sibilla reluctantly follows him, aware of the fact that her husband will otherwise insist on his legal right to have custody of their son. As the book closes, the protagonist understands both the right and the price of freedom. But sacrifices too have limits and such limits begin when a human being is forced to surrender his own being, his aspirations, his individuality—all the things that affirm his worth and importance. This realization allows her to choose the only decent alternative: to leave her husband and son and make her life somewhere else.

At the center of *Una donna*, as in most of her other novels, there is a basic problem presented in the form of a conflict between dreams and hopes and the repulsive manner in which they are simply destroyed. The theme of the book is allowed to grow gradually, enriched along the way by an ideological component that contributes a startling intensity. Such ideology, which has much in common with Ibsen's, is given substance by the violence, the disappointments, and the tragedies that engulf the heroine without destroying her. On the contrary the violence to which the protagonist is subjected and is forced to endure is precisely what strengthens her resolve to become an individual. In short, Sibilla reaches a new awareness of her condition by living through the experiences of life: her loss of virginity, her father's total incomprehension of her needs as a woman, her husband's tyranny, and her attempted suicide. Having lived through this, Sibilla realizes the dire urgency of crushing the petty traditions that have made life so unbearable for her and of making it possible for men and women to have a finer understanding of their uniqueness and individuality. In this sense, then, Sibilla's decision is at once personal and unique, for it is a kind of proclamation that women are human beings and, like men, are entitled to a free existence that will permit them to fulfill themselves according to their potentials. This makes *Una donna* an anti-Establishment work much like, say, Pirandello's *L'esclusa* or *Il fu Mattia Pascal*. The three novels begin with a situation set in a traditional social and ideological structure which comes increasingly under fire, if only in an indirect fashion. Existing social institutions, marriage particularly, are exposed for what they often are: empty, meaningless arrangements, inadequate at best and repressive at worst, and as such subject to scrutiny to determine just how they are responsive to human needs. Without discounting the obvious autobiographical character of *Una donna*, one must see it also as an inspired attempt to force an intellectual confrontation with a system that since time immemorial has constantly been guilty of discrimination against the "second sex," forcing it to endure the tyranny of men.

Considerable pathos pervades the book. Theme and style are admirably fused in a way that, for all the polemical character of the story told, prevents *Una donna* from being turned into an angry, raucous work. The confessional tone and approach are most effective, particularly because their personal quality is appropriate in depicting the ripening process of the heroine from an innocent, naïve young girl to a disillusioned adult still able to look at life with a rare philosophical detachment. Experience is what Sibilla feeds herself on, and it is experience that enables her to become wise and compassionate about the frailty of human existence. Through pain, she becomes conscious of the anguish of living; but pain nobly endured gives her the strength to conclude that unorthodox decisions have got to be made when precious issues are at stake. Here perhaps is one of the magnetic qualities of *Una donna*: written well over a half century ago, it addresses itself to the impelling need to find meaning and purpose in the otherwise unpredictable affair that life is.

5

Alfredo Panzini: The Bourgeois Novel

The life and work of Alfredo Panzini straddle two centuries: yet, although he reached his maturity in our century, he remained ideologically and culturally tied to the *fin de siècle*. A bourgeois by birth, he was a bourgeois in his work; with respect to his training and background, as well as to his orientation in belletristic matters, he was a classicist. He revered the classics, he was inspired by them, and he sought to retain (and sporadically improve) the tradition of which he was a product.

He was born in Senigallia, on the eastern seaboard of the Italian peninsula, in 1863. His father was a physician and a moderately well-to-do landowner who lost his small fortune at the gambling table. Having completed his secondary education in his hometown, Alfredo was awarded a scholarship at the Venetian boarding school of Foscarini, thanks to the personal intervention of an official of the Prefecture of Senigallia. After graduating from the *liceo* he enrolled at the University of Bologna, where he studied under one of Italy's most prestigious poets and scholars, Giosue Carducci. In 1886 Panzini graduated with a thesis on Macaronic poetry, a special type of poetry distinguished for its humorous language, whose structure and syntax is Latin but whose words are both Latin and Italian—with Latin endings! He won a national competition for a teaching position, and was assigned first to Castellamare di Stabia near Naples, then to Imola, and later on, thanks to the interest of his mentor Carducci, to Milan, where he remained until 1917. At that time, unable to withstand the sorrow of the loss of his only son Umbertino, who had died in 1910, he moved to Rome. In 1928 he retired; one year later he was named to the Accademia d'Italia, newly revived by Mussolini. He remained active in journalism until the day of his death, April 10, 1939.

The pattern of Panzini's trajectory is all too familiar, particularly in terms of his education. What is unusual is the fact that his attraction to teaching seems to have been due not so much to vocational but to practical reasons.

Trained by a great classicist, it was only natural that early in his university studies Panzini should develop great sensitivity toward classical literature, Latin and Italian. His reverence for Homer, Catullus, Hesiod, Vergil, Boiardo, and Ariosto (to mention a few of his favorite authors) is reflected page after page in the numerous books he wrote during a busy life, books full of descriptions of nature and rural life. His style, often worked with a proverbial fine artist's file, was carefully chiseled so as to translate into literature the idyllic and pastoral world he longed for. The words he used, the themes that recur in his literary production, the scene and moods he was able to create on the printed page, suggest the unique flavor of his native landscape of Romagna he deeply loved. To be sure, his labors are not always successful: at times one feels a kind of pedantic, overly strained technique that destroys the feeling of spontaneity he sought to project. But there is more than that: his books bring out a tendency to flee the "unlivable cities," a pronounced preference for the peace and calm of the countryside. Panzini obviously identified himself with a less chaotic, more firmly structured age. His deep concern for what must have seemed to him an erosion of traditional values is reflected time and again in his concept of a society tightly organized around the family. Similarly, his respect for his nation, his eagerness to see it restored to a position of greatness, indicate the character of a man whose values were those of the educated middle class, regrettably unable to accept the less selfish, nobler aspirations of the liberal and leftist groups. Panzini's love of family, God, and country, his sense of wonderment toward nature, his solid respect for the vital functions of the woman are commendable and admirable, were it not for the fact that, as presented in his work, they glorify the life of the bourgeoisie, committed to order and the preservation of social and political institutions, particularly jealous of its power and prerogatives. Behind this façade of respectability, as is often the case, was another less attractive sight Panzini's sensitivity recognized but was unable, incapable, or unwilling to confront: the exploitation of the working class, the repressive policies at home and the imperialistic course in foreign policy, the intellectual and moral corruption that were to lead to the emergence and victory of fascism in the 1920s. He "does not succeed in shaping and communicating his emotions and his poetic images," in Benedetto Croce's words ". . . if not through a mask he has placed on his face, the mask of someone who does not understand the fraud that is life, and the reason why men and women are what they are, and, since he declares that he doesn't understand, he feels superior to him who thinks he understands."

The image that emerges out of the books Panzini wrote is less that of a novelist than of a perennial "tourist" in the best sense of the term, an eager commentator of life: hence his numerous bicycle trips to the eastern coast of Italy, to towns and hamlets his classical readings had taught him to love. His excursions provided him with ample inspiration for his short stories and essays, while his love for the past gave further impetus to his propensity to write fables, the most escapist of literary activities. The characters he created to people his books are all, to varying degrees, projections of himself: rational, considerate, decent, prone to skepticism, neither excessively inventive nor profound—people, in short, facing the dawn of a new era, yet incapable of responding to it, unprepared to meet the challenges of the new times and the changes of mores and values that inevitably accompany such times. "If we scrutinize [Panzini's] opinions," noted, tartly, Benedetto Croce, "his contradictory judgments, his contrasting feelings, I am afraid we cannot find anything but a great fear of a world on the move, and an uneasiness that may come from this motion to his own tranquillity and his own comfort." Panzini chose the only viable way out of his predicament by filtering his experience through autobiographical lenses, thus giving his ideas about the world's consistency and credibility. "The author's interest," observed one of his earliest and most perceptive, if overly generous critics, Renato Serra, "is not in [his] characters, whose story he happens to recount: it is in the story of his own heart; his narrative is above all a long and thoughtful soliloquy, now and then varied by light characters."

Panzini wrote an extraordinary number of books, and versatility was unquestionably his trademark: essays, short stories, pseudohistorical works, novels, and an engaging *Dizionario moderno* through which he sought to enrich his language by compiling and explaining the many words that had been drawn from other languages and dialects and had become part of colloquial Italian. Only toward the last years of his life did Panzini's work score great success with the general public, even though his writings had appeared regularly in such middle-brow reviews as *L'Illustrazione italiana* and *La Nuova Antologia.* As for the critics, that was another story. He received constant attention from them, even though some, such as Luigi Russo and Benedetto Croce, could not always be counted among his admirers. In the twenties such a critic as Luigi Tonelli, in his *Alla ricerca della personalità,* named Panzini along with Grazia Deledda and Luigi Pirandello as a "writer most worthily celebrated." Croce, on the other hand, complained in a stinging essay that for some twenty years Panzini had sought to enlarge his public by sacrificing quality, and charged him with working "mechanically," and of "growing frivolity and vacuousness." The author himself was not unaware of the dangers of spreading himself too thin by doing too much: what with his regular teaching assignment, his extra course taught at a Polytechnical Institute in Milan, and private tutoring lessons to increase his meager stipend, he complained, in a letter to his good friend and fellow writer Marino Moretti in 1919: "I am tired of working. No working man has worked more than me. Useless work, perhaps, but work nevertheless." Like a score of writers before and after him (Balzac and Dostoievski, to mention just two), Panzini discovered the terror of turning himself into a kind of automaton desperately trying to keep abreast with his publishing commitments. But what of those critics who admired him: what did they see in his writings that elicited their respect and esteem? The question may best be answered if we bear in mind that in an era that was beginning to react both to the "sloppy" writing of the post-*veristi* and the gilded prose of d'Annunzio, readers must have found some comfort in a man of letters whose roots were in the classical tradition, who had a feeling for style and who cared for his métier. Interestingly enough, his acceptance was made easier by a growing tendency to receive sympathetically lovely stories, prose poems which, like a single perfect, precious diamond, would most completely give life to the illumination of the poet. In an era of Dannunzian rhetoric, which had followed a type of novel not many would find palatable because of its frequent starkness and brutal candor, it must have seemed comforting to read a writer who could be witty and charming without being bombastic or offensive.

What kind of writer was Panzini? Judging from his short stories, it can be said that he was, to put it simply, an uncomplicated fabulist, a melancholy *narrateur* who could depict the pathos of life, but not its tragedy; who could dramatically present his unhappiness with the present but could not be aroused by the indignities that produced wretchedness; who could delicately and convincingly address himself to the wonderful quality of life of yesteryear without understanding the fact that the past appears beautiful to us simply because our historical perspective makes us forget its dark and rainy days.

A simple illustration will suffice. The short story "Le ostriche di San Damiano" [The Oysters of Saint Damiano] tells of a teacher who goes to a fancy restaurant, the kind he cannot really afford, and is more or less coerced by the waiter to order a meal beyond his means, even though the oysters he is served are "on the house" in celebration of the patron saint of the day. The owner, we soon discover, had been one of the teacher's former students who had failed in Latin and Italian. The professor is understandably embarrassed: the restauranteur, on the other hand, is very grateful to his former teacher. The failing grade he received in school was the event that finally persuaded his father of his son's lack of interest in academic studies. As a result, he was sent to a well-known training school in Switzerland where he acquired the skill that made possible his success.

The story, narrated in a light, unpretentious manner, is in a sense typical of the frothiness, humor, and simplicity of Panzini. But not all his stories have a humorous theme. "Padre e figlio" [Father and son], published in 1911 in the volume *Fiabe della virtú*, is a tale of the deep discord between two generations, a theme whose implications are as contemporary as we are likely to find. Domenico is a highly successful farmer, renowned all over his region for the skill and excellent results achieved by his method of raising cows and working the soil. His marriage has been a disaster, and shortly after the birth of his son Marco, he separates from his wife, who dies shortly afterward. Marco is enrolled in a fine boarding school where he becomes an outstanding student whose incredible mind permits him to commit to memory entire passages of the books he reads. Everyone predicts a brilliant future for the youngster, an opinion confirmed by his excellence in the law school to which he has been admitted and from which he attains his degree. Much to his father's dismay, however, Marco chooses not to open a law office, but rather becomes a writer. The people of the town admire his dedication to his chosen vocation; his father, on the other hand, bitterly resents the fact that his son's commitment to write prevents him from taking over the family's successful business.

As time goes on, Marco visits his father less and less regularly, except when he is ready (as his father complains) "to give birth to his book." One day Marco, now forty years old, returns home, falls ill, and dies. His death proves to be a traumatic experience for Domenico, who begins divesting himself of his property, donating it to charitable organizations while planning to transform his house, and particularly the study of his late son, into a kind of shrine. "Then," concludes Panzini, "time passed and people spoke no more about Marco, the hero, than about the monument and the cypress tree."

"Padre e figlio" is a moving story, pervaded by pathos, tightly constructed around the conflict between material and nonmaterial values, the misunderstanding between the old and the new generations, and the insensitivity of those who see only in the accumulation of wealth man's ultimate goal, his *raison d'être*.

The awareness of what nowaday is usually called "the generation gap," is a leitmotif of much of Panzini's literary production. As early as 1893, in his book *Il libro dei Morti* [The book of the dead], one of the characters, Giacomo, confesses his sense of dislocation by saying: "I am out of place in this society. I am lost in it." This feeling is essentially what motivates Panzini to insist on looking to the past for his roots but also, alas, as the only way to avoid the unpleasantness and the difficulties of the present. We find this in his short stories, and we find it in most, if not all, the longer works (generally hybrids of fiction, history, travel commentary, personal reminiscences, erudition, and so forth) as *La Lanterna di Diogene* [Diogenes' lantern] (1907) and *Viaggio di un povero letterato* [Voyage of a poor man of letters] (1918).

Of the many *novels* (the term is used here for the want of a better one) Panzini wrote, *La Madonna di Mamà* seems to come closest to the traditional concept of the genre. Moreover, the author himself had a special regard for this work, as evidenced from the thorough revisions to which he subjected it when he prepared it for subsequent editions.

Traditional in every sense, the book has a simple theme, one dear to Panzini for it was drawn from his own experience: the struggle and the pain endured by a young man who leaves his native town for the city, where he will shed his provincial attitudes and ideas and will gain his manhood. The novel represents one of Panzini's efforts to understand the present, with all its complexities, without seeking refuge in the past. At last Panzini faces squarely the dislocation brought about by the First World War and, by extension, all wars, while simultaneously following the young protagonist's attempt to be absorbed, accepted by, and integrated into urban society.

The protagonist of the story is Aquilino who, having achieved his diploma, accepts a position with a wealthy aristocratic family as the private tutor of their bright, spoiled, but engaging child Bobby. The first few months in the new position are particularly difficult for Aquilino, who tries to find his way in a totally new, mysterious, and even alien milieu and to establish a productive rapport with his charge. Fortunately, Bobby is not only extremely intelligent but both cunning and skillful in his polemics with his tutor, whose weaknesses and contradictions he manages to exploit to his own advantage, thus making their relationship lively and full of surprises. Eventually the two become good friends and learn to get along remarkably well. Aquilino himself proves to be a decent and patient teacher who has the sympathy of his employers, the marquis Ippolito and his wife donna Barberina, who for a while becomes his mistress.

The story leads to the troubling months preceding the outbreak of World War I and the political crisis in Italy, a crisis that brings about a split into two factions, one for, the other violently opposed to the war and Italy's participation in it. Aquilino's hawkish stance is not really traceable so much to his political beliefs as to his love for Edith, an English governess in the employ of the same family. Both become involved in the prowar movement. One day they are caught in an antiwar demonstration; fortunately, they succeed in escaping the fury of the mob, and take refuge in a nearby hotel. There their relationship, which has been of a most formal sort, blossoms into a carnal one. As the book ends, Aquilino takes his leave from Edith as he departs for the service.

La Madonna di Mamà, as even this synopsis makes evident, is not a very exciting book. Yet, it is as typical of the best of Panzini's art as any other novel he wrote. There is, for example, a detectable intrusion on his part in the novel itself by way of a gentle surface irony and by the humor that subtly pervades the story. Here at last we get a sense of something happening, changing and evolving, a rare quality in Panzini's otherwise static work; we also feel something of the changes in the personal relationships of the various characters: Bobby, Aquilino, donna Barberina, Edith. And we sense a small measure of the historical changes Italy underwent during the troubling pre-World War I months, particularly with respect to the politics of the extreme right and left. But there are many disturbing features that tend to rob the novel of the excitement it should have: the characters are drawn without much depth; the events are by and large too casually depicted. Panzini seems to be an artist more at home with watercolors than oils, with a small canvas rather than a large one; with common situations that are easily definable. It is no wonder that Pietro Pancrazi once shrewdly remarked that "[Panzini's] characters may make us think about the soles [of a shoe]: there is one side, and there is the other side, but you never see either one."

Structurally, too, the novel is both revealing and typical, particularly in terms of its author's ability to compose a sustained narrative. *La Madonna di Mamà* is divided into twenty-six fairly brief chapters, most of which bear a title: both in treatment and length, they seem to be almost self-contained units that could be read and enjoyed often independently of the whole. Other elements typical of Panzini may again be found in *La Madonna di Mamà*: a gentle irony and a modest, but persistent moralizing of the Manzoni type. Thus, for example, after talking with the Marquis don Ippolito di Torrechiara, Aquilino, the author concludes, was not displeased by his comments, "because when man finds himself in some serious difficulties, he is happy if others prove to him that perfection exists neither on earth nor in the heavens." Or, after still another conversation with the marquis, the author comments: "You see! When I was a child, my mother—bless her soul—used to say: 'the grass

I WANT grows nowhere except in the Pope's garden.' It is obvious that it no longer grows there, either."

Episodic, skeptical, mildly ironical, a perennial if restrained pessimist, Panzini loved the past more than the present and constructed much of his literary work around the theme of yesteryear. He was a gentle writer—never haunted by his imagination, always eager to reach the general public, which he knew to be ill-prepared for difficult books. His attitudes and his conception of what his task should be unavoidably made writing of some depth impossible or uncertain at best. And that is why Panzini seldom displeased any of his readers and never truly challenged his critics. He belongs to an era of *crepuscolarismo*, a period of soft lights and humble visions. He is at best a pleasant narrator, at worst a simplistic moralizer: he was, as one recent critic aptly put it, a writer born not "to create facts and characters, but to hide behind them." "His goal," continues Claudio Marabini, "does not change: he will always look for a man, a small virtue, a soul. He never ceases putting off that searching look, ready to ask whomever he meets: 'What is there inside of you, in the most jealous shadow? And you, what are you looking for?' . . . This is why he never succeeded in writing either history or novels, which require a firm ideal."

6

Giuseppe A. Borgese: The Ideological Void

The history of world letters offers numerous examples of poets and novelists whose careers include serious, productive, and meaningful activity as critics. One thinks immediately of Shelley, Keats, Coleridge, Wordsworth, Matthew Arnold, Leopardi, Goethe, Carducci, and the contemporary Valéry and T. S. Eliot, among others. The reverse, the nucleus of professional critics who have tried their hand at creative writing is slimmer and far less impressive. In general, we tend to value what a poet has to say about the art he practises because it can illuminate the mystery of the creative process. On the other hand, by and large, by disposition, training, and inclination professional critics seem to be better suited to analyze rather than invent, to be sensitive of the beauty and power of poetry rather than capable of forging out of reality an invented world that illuminates life and man's condition. Rarely are such critics haunted by the demon of their imagination, and even more seldom can they forget their professional status and allow themselves to be the willing victims of their fantasy. So diverse are the scopes and techniques of the two activities that, however finely they may be pursued, it is safe to say that, like good wines, they do not easily mix.

In some ways at least, Giuseppe A. Borgese is possibly something of a minor exception: he practised the two arts with great skill and competence and for a while, with equal devotion. This in and by itself would not make him an important writer. He is remembered here despite his imperfections as a novelist because it would be difficult to neglect his part in providing an example of how the novel should change. He sought to rejuvenate the genre by a process of deprovincialization that was to be achieved mainly by introducing themes, moods, and techniques he had studied closely as a critic of great European writing, particularly the French and Russian writers.

Academic by training, Borgese was generous and perceptive in his examination of his contemporaries: Giovanni Verga, Federigo Tozzi, Alberto Moravia, and Guido Piovene, for example, received his accolades. The fact that the first three are recognized as classics underscores Borgese's excellent taste and sure eye. Time and again he insisted and put into practise the concept that the novel should become a medium through which the writer could offer a synthesis of his own era. "What this novel tells," wrote Pietro Pancrazi apropos of *Rubè*, "the contrasts hinted therein, the ideas debated in it, are things that at last matter to us." "For Borgese," adds Carlo Bo, "it was no longer possible to make use of the classical formula of the novel to attempt a diagnosis of his own time. A good critic by instinct but a bad one when the time came to measure his own talent and disposition. . . . [he] thought [it] appropriate to dramatize the century's new malaise in the figure of Filippo Rubè, forgetting immediately that it was necessary to proceed in a totally different way, avoiding first of all all traditional tableaux and [man's] faulty memory of human experience."

The biography of Giuseppe A. Borgese is rich in activities that literally run the spectrum: from scholarship to journalism; from criticism to poetry and fiction; from a nationalistic involvement in his country's politics to a statesmanlike position in world affairs. He was born in Polizzi Generosa near Palermo, on November 12, 1882, and was educated first at the University of Palermo and then at the University of Florence, a city where Borgese spent a long, happy, and productive period. He began writing verse as a youth. At the age of eighteen founded his own "little magazine" *Scintilla*, and at twenty-two the more serious but equally short-lived *Hermes*. He wrote some fine literary criticism for some years after he had graduated, much of it published in the authoritative Milanese daily *Il corriere della sera,* and collected his articles and reviews in three volumes bearing the titles *La vita e il libro* [Life and books] (1910–28), *Studi di letterature moderne* [Studies of modern literatures] (1920), and *Tempo di edificare* [Time to build] (1924).

Books on political questions, *Italia e Germania* (1915), *La guerra delle idee* [The war of ideas] (1916), *L'Italia e la Nuova Alleanza* [Italy and the new alliance] (1917), among others, proved to be just as important to Borgese as his literary criticism—much of his own fiction was to show his awareness of politics and his obsession with political intrigues. His scholarly *Storia della critica romantica* [History of romantic criticism] (1905) and his study of Pascoli were highly praised by such a close reader as Benedetto Croce who, disappointed and even piqued by the subsequent critical posture of his disciple, became his most bitter and severest critic until his death.

In 1931 Borgese refused to sign the oath of allegiance to the Fascist party required of all university professors. He left Italy in a self-imposed exile and took up residence in the United States, where he was named professor of Italian and Comparative Literature at Smith College and, subsequently, at the Universities of California and Chicago. In the early forties, together with such inveterate anti-Fascists as Count Carlo Sforza and Gaetano Salvemini, he organized the liberal-republican Mazzini Society. In the last years of his life, he became an articulate spokesman for world government and internal cooperation and disarmament. He died in Fiesole in 1952.

A glimpse at his biographical events reinforces the suspicion that the most celebrated and successful fictional character Borgese created, Rubè (1921), is largely a projection of the author himself. With his maker, Rubè shares his diverse interests, his Sicilian temperament, his flamboyant expression, the acentricity of his drives, his unchanneled idealism—the very qualities, one is bound to notice, that ultimately were responsible for Borgese's failure to make his mark as a novelist, a critic, or a political leader. As fiction,

Rubè, the best and most representative work he wrote, is marred by flaws unanimously acknowledged and discussed by generations of readers. It is difficult not to be irritated by its baroque style, the occasional incoherence and artificiality of its images, its grandiloquence and virtuosity.

These views, justifiably held by many of those who have lived with *Rubè* presumably long enough to begin understanding it, are not really sufficient to enable us to come to grips with what the novel tries to say and what it attempts to do. Luigi Russo states that the book "gives us a significant and dramatic representation of the *homo novus*," himself a product of the "heroic-individualistic doctrines in the moment of their encounter with a new philosophy of life, a new faith that showed the vanity and despair of every form of intellectualism." In a very special way, Rubè is the character that epitomizes the distress and confusion of a generation that found itself living through a world conflict it had hoped would resolve some of the major problems afflicting humanity, only to awaken to the bitter, desperate realization that it had not; indeed, as we all discovered, it created new ones that eventually led to World War II.

In his analysis of *Rubè*, the late Domenico Vittorini remarked that it is "a novel about a young man whose power of analysis is so overdeveloped that he is thereby rendered unfit to live. In this sense, Rubè is the symbol of the decadent European youth that is exemplified in the doctrine of the superman. Rubè, however, is not the follower of d'Annunzio, but his antithesis." Aside from the doubtful implication that an overdeveloped power of analysis must inevitably be detrimental to a "normal" existence, it is hard to disagree in the main with Vittorini's characterization of the novel. What we are beginning to perceive, even with a limited perspective of four decades, is that *Rubè* is less a well-made novel, or a well-written narrative, than a work that anticipates certain vital trends in literature and politics alike that were to blossom in the years following its publication, while simultaneously offering an accurate reflection of the mood of despair pervading the first decades of our century. In yet another way, the central character of Borgese's tale is also what might be called the antihero, after the definition offered some years ago by Sean O'Faolain in his book *The Vanishing Hero*:

> The Anti-Hero is a much less tidy and comfortable concept than the social Hero since—being deprived of social sanctions and definitions—he is always trying to define himself, to find his own sanctions. He is always represented as groping, puzzled, morose, mocking, frustrated, isolated in his manful or blundering attempts to establish his own personal suprasocial codes. . . . He is sometimes ridiculous through lack of perspicacity, accentuated by an attractive if foolhardy personal courage. Whether he is weak, brave, brainy, or bewildered, he is always out on his own.

If Rubè is indeed constantly analyzing his feelings and thoughts, haunted by Hamletian doubts, he has little in common with the metaphysical probings of Pirandello's characters. Whereas Pirandello's heroes are engaged in a dialectic dialogue with their fellowmen on the nature of existence, the question of the multiplicity of personality, and the fundamentally alienating nature of human relations, Rubè is actually involved in a painful monologue (that only infrequently turns into a dialogue) concerning the sincerity of *his* acts, the true motivation of what *he* does as a rational animal. He is therefore presented as a human being perennially buffeted by the capricious whims of Fate, a man totally incapable of fulfilling himself because he has neither true ideals nor the moral and intellectual strength to formulate worthwhile goals for his existence. From beginning to end, he remains therefore a person torn between what he ought to do and what he has enough conviction to do. His conflict springs from the fact that the gap between the two proves to be substantially larger than he had anticipated, too large in fact for him to bridge easily. In desperation, Rubè resorts to constructing a personality for himself, not in terms of what he *wants* to be, but of what people *expect* him to be, a pragmatist *sui generis*. It is in this respect that Rubè may be called the prototype of the spineless, "indifferent" hero that emerges in full force in the fiction of Alberto Moravia.

Rubè is a young Sicilian who has "descended upon Rome," armed not only with the customary letters of recommendation but with the "logical mind capable of splitting a hair into four, an oratorical fire that burned his opponents argument to the bone, and a certain faith that he had great things in him." The initial presentation of such distressing personal characteristics is of key importance in understanding the substance of the personality of the hero and Borgese's own ironical resolution of the personal dilemma of his protagonist, as we shall see. Meanwhile, we penetrate the personality of Rubè by following his actions: an avowed interventionist (the novel is set in 1914), he volunteers his services and requests to be sent to the future battle lines. Once the war is declared, Rubè, equally afraid of war and death, is wounded during an air raid and sent back to the rear lines. Colonel Berti extends the hospitality of his home to him during his convalescence, and there he meets the colonel's young daughter Eugenia, who nurses him back to health, readily succumbs to his demands, and becomes his mistress. Back at the front he acquits himself well enough to be decorated, but his nervous condition makes it imperative that he be sent home and discharged. Since he wishes to continue serving his country, he is sent to Paris as a member of a military-technical commission. In the French capital he is introduced to the salon of Madame Celestina Lambert, the exquisite and attractive wife of a general.

At the end of the war, Rubè returns to his country, marries Eugenia, and settles down to a post with Adsum, a large metallurgical concern in Milan. Shortly afterward, however, he sides with the workers' legitimate demands for better working conditions and wage increases and loses his position. In a moment of despair, he goes to a gambling casino with a friend. There, in a manner reminiscent of Pirandello's Mattia Pascal, he wins a considerable sum of money. He decides to go away for a period of rest and, quite by accident, he stops at the Isola Bella, where by coincidence and without his knowing it, Celestina is vacationing. Rubè's extraordinary personal charm proves too much to resist, and Celestina willingly becomes his mistress. Several days later, the general visits his wife, learns of her affair, and requests her to return to Paris at once. Rubè and Celestina decide to go on a last outing on the lake before separating. A sudden storm capsizes the small boat, throwing the two occupants against a cliff, an accident that proves fatal to Celestina. Rubè is accused of murder but successfully proves his innocence. After the trial, he departs to join his expectant wife whom he has asked to meet him at Bologna. There, shortly after getting off the train, he quite accidentally finds himself carried away by a stormy left-wing group staging an antigovernment demonstration, and loses his life when he is crushed by a policeman's horse.

Like his life, Rubè's death is an irony: just as he had lived a purposeless and meaningless life, so he must die an unnecessary death while participating, against his will, in a demonstration whose true purpose, much like everything else in his life, he does not understand and with whose cause he cannot possibly identify himself. It is not without its own symbolic meaning that Rubè dies clutching in his hands the black flag of the Fascists and the red one of the Communists, the two opposing political forces representing the extremism whose first victim is an innocent spectator.

Significant, too, is the fact that the novel is set between 1914 and 1920, two crucial dates in modern Italian history, for it was in the wake of the First World War and in the ensuing political and economic uncertainty that fascism emerged. But the political atmosphere of the period is always kept as a convenient sort of backdrop in the more dramatic conflict that looms large. Simply stated, it is a conflict that involves a whole nation, incapable—like Rubè who thereby becomes its spokesman and representative specimen—of preserving the democratic way of life that was still within its grasp.

Rubè is the child of his time: he is the empty and purposeless automaton we find again in Moravia's *Gli indifferenti* (1929; *The Time of Indifference*, N.Y., 1953), the man looking everywhere for sincerity, truth, and the vitality of life he himself lacks. By his own confession, Rubè belongs to "that most unhappy intellectual, provincial bourgeoisie, spoiled by an education of all or nothing, vitiated by the taste of definitive ascensions from which panoramas are contemplated." "Our hands," he says at one point, "have no callouses; our tendons are weak; we can't grasp a spade or a shovel; all we can grasp is the void." Such a revealing self-analysis, negative a judgment as it no doubt is, makes Rubè a figure with a large relevance to our contemporary predicament. His words and acts never rise above the plane of empty and basically meaningless gestures, automatic reflexes of a man who confronts but never once comes to terms with the crises of his life. By doing so, he becomes the epitome of the malaise of his own generation, troubled and confused by a changing world, an absurd man *sui generis*, an *homme revolté* not by what he sees but by what he does, thinks, and says. For him, everything is nothing, but the very dread of nothingness is also what haunts him day and night. The failure of man to become and thus *be* a human being is the very essence of Pirandellian dilemma, of course. But in the world of the Sicilian playwright an answer, whether by self-deceit or by withdrawal into a make-believe world, is possible. Rubè undergoes several traumatic experiences before he can hear, from the mouth of his friend Federico, a devastating appraisal of his condition. "You've made the mistake of applying your terrible logic to your own life even more than to your client's affairs. But as a result of hammering at yourself with your logic, you've shattered yourself to bits. . . . Accept your shortcomings in a tolerant spirit." It is a remark that warrants heeding even in the world of our own generation.

7

Voices from the Provinces: Grazia Deledda and Marino Moretti

Grazia Deledda

Like Verga, Capuana, Serao, and a host of other Italian writers of the closing decades of the nineteenth century, Grazia Deledda has traditionally, and I think in some ways unfairly, been labeled a *regionalist*, a term that as we shall see hardly does full justice to her work or explains the nature of her world. It is true, as even a cursory reading of her books makes evident, that an imposing part of her narrative writing—particularly in the early part of her literary career—is set in her native Sardinia. The choice of remote, forbidding, and primitive settings was deliberate, and what is more important, never an end in itself. Deledda always tried to be close to, and write from her own experience, from the kind of life she knew best and felt most comfortable with—and when she did not, her failures are conspicuous. This observation can also be extended to her brief encounter with socialism, whose programs were being derided and demeaned in every possible way by the Establishment at the turn of the century, and to her posture on such social questions as divorce, which is the theme of one of her novels, titled aptly enough *Dopo il divorzio* (1902; *After the Divorce*, N.Y., 1905). As Deledda matured, her sensitive knowledge of the traditions and customs of Sardinia became smoothly interwoven with plot and characterization to the point of becoming an indistinguishable part of the fabric of her narrative.

86

Folklore achieved then an undeniable functionality, giving her tableaux their special colors and illuminating the problematical temperament of her characters. Her descriptions of Sardinian life and geography are a fitting backdrop against which the loneliness, anguish, doubts, and emotions of her characters take on a different dimension. This is particularly true in the novels Deledda composed after leaving her native island in 1900 when, now a married woman, she established residence in Rome. Distance and time enabled her to "see" and remember her Sardinia which became, as Deledda herself was to confess, "a country of myths and legends." Domenico Vittorini put it another way when he remarked that she "dedicated her long career to the passionate evocation of the landscape of her beloved island, its customs, and picturesque inhabitants, often observed and studied in actual life in the fields and towns near Nuoro." This special treatment permits the reader to come away from her books remembering not so much specific places in Sardinia but moods most effectively conjured up by her fantasy. Through the descriptions of rituals and unique customs of the island, we also derive a feeling of the rhythm of a life cut off from peninsular happenings. The primitive nature of the locales of Deledda's narratives is well in tune with the basic feelings she dramatized over and again: hatred, fear, love, remorse, and an inescapable sense of fatalism. The harsh, muted Sardinian landscape thus helps to define the fundamental dilemmas of its people, their unique half-mystical, half-fatalistic way of looking at the world. By the same token, the inflexibility of the social order of the island and its system of values represent the realities one cannot slight. It is in this sense that Deledda's Sardinia is turned from a purely geographic entity into a poetic one, much like Verga's Aci Trezza, with its special tension and dramatic elements.

Grazia Deledda was born in Nuoro (Sardinia) in 1871 into a moderately well-to-do middle-class family and never went beyond her secondary school training. Tutored privately for some years, she showed neither an inclination for, nor an interest in academic studies. She was an exemplary eclectic: she read a great deal (her range goes from the poet Prati to Victor Hugo, from Chateaubriand to Sue and Dumas Sr.) but with little discrimination. She admired the writers of her own time, particularly Fogazzaro, Carducci, and d'Annunzio, was to a limited extent influenced by their example, but seldom imitated them. At the age of twenty she confessed with angelic candor that the great classics such as Manzoni, Tasso, and Boccaccio made her yawn and want to go to sleep—a comment hardly calculated to draw the approval of her critics, many of whom have since reproached her inadequate education.

The drive to write came not from a wish to emulate or surpass her literary models, but from within. Perhaps, as she confessed in the semiautobiographical *Cosima* (published posthumously), it was a "subterranean force," or perhaps it was an unconscious desire to retell, in her own way, some of the fables that had helped her to pass happily many a long winter evening in her childhood. However this may be, she began publishing at the age of seventeen. Her first poems and short stories brought much consternation to her native city: her characters, drawn from reality, could easily be identified and for this she was verbally chastised by her readers. Eventually, after appearing in several magazines for women, Deledda found her manner—somber, simple, modest. She remained faithful to her narrative mode until the end, a fact that impelled some of her critics to insist on the gray, monotonous character of her writing. By the time she died in 1936, she had produced over forty volumes, had won both the Nobel Prize for literature in 1926 and the admiration and esteem of the international audience.

There is something refreshing about Deledda's art, even as we view it from our modest historical perspective. Next to the mysticism of Fogazzaro, the baroque sensuality of d'Annunzio, and the sentimentality of Pascoli, the aspirations and problems of Deledda's characters are genuine, if somewhat limited. But we will not understand them—with their definition of life and the simplistic answers they propose—unless we are willing to accept them on their own terms: poor, and in some ways noble peasants, coming to grips with reality as best they can. The forces driving their lives and ultimately responsible for their choices and their results are not unusual: indeed, the simplicity of Deledda's characters, with their social and intellectual limitations, is what enables them to respond as they do to a kind of subterranean instinct, a dogmatic code of ethics they fully accept. The basic problems they face are ultimately and invariably translated in terms of good versus evil, reason versus capriciousness, false values versus enduring ones, sensual love versus caritas. Uneducated, submissive, and, by bourgeois standards, unsophisticated in the ways of life, Deledda's characters manage to understand at least the seriousness of the issues they confront if not always the substance of the alternatives open to them. Their cultural tradition is at once their source of strength and their limitation from which they derive a kind of elemental comfort, an awareness that the human condition dooms them to being constant participants of a self-repeating drama that offers no truly satisfactory conclusion.

In many of Deledda's novels we follow the development of the protagonists over an extended period of time. At times, as in *La madre* (1920; *The Mother*, N.Y., 1923), the crisis they confront comes to a resolution within the space of two days; invariably, they accept their condition stoically. But, as E. Allen McCormick remarks, their "moral struggle is rarely of tragic dimensions." The dice appear to be constantly loaded against them: what we get is, at best, drama of a limited yet powerful sort.

Grazia Deledda's literary production has conveniently been divided into two distinct periods. Arnaldo Bocelli, in a perceptive essay written upon her death, identified them by pointing out how the vision of life is transcendental in the first phase and immanent in the second. In her early novels (1896–1920), God is presented as a kind of implacable, biblical dispenser of justice, "in that we are all sinners and there is no salvation either here or beyond."

The notable novels of the first creative "moment" are *Elias Portulu* (1903), *Cenere* (1903; *Ashes*, N.Y., 1908),

L'edera [Ivy] (1908), *Colombi e sparvieri* [Doves and sparrowhawks] (1912), and *Canne al vento* [Reeds to the wind] (1913). The second period opens in 1920 with *La madre* and *Il segreto dell'uomo solitario* [The secret of the solitary man] (1921), both of which remain the finest work of Deledda's later years. In the novels brought out between 1921 and 1936 the role of property and the obsession with material things, key elements of the work of the *veristi* which had been Deledda's models, undergo considerable deemphasis. Love is no longer the sensual and potentially destructive force that it was, but is a restrained, almost religious feeling, a bond between one person and another. Through compassion, one attains a finer understanding of human sorrows, and such a different concept of love brings about notable changes in Deledda's narrative. The themes of her later books receive a more consciously intellectual treatment; the settings, so vividly depicted in the earlier novels, suddenly become secondary. We begin moving in a more abstract land, outside geography and time. However much such novels strive to broaden their meaning and application, they are unquestionably less effective and powerful than the early ones. Deledda herself must have perceived where her real strength as a novelist was, for she soon returned to the fatalism and the haunting pessimism of her "regional," veristic period.

Deledda's early novels as *Le colpe altrui* [Someone else's faults] (1914), *L'incendio nell'oliveto* [Fire in the olive grove] (1918), and even *La madre* (1920) may be seen, after Eurialo De Michelis's suggestion, as extreme efforts "to grasp once more in rigorously moral terms a drama, which is still [the same as] that of Elias Portulu, between love and duty. . . ." In point of fact, love is very much at the center of most of Deledda's novels, a love presented as a source of conflict, now love-fatalism, now love-remorse, now love-guilt—an experience, in short, that brings about a profound sense of shame and which, for mysterious reasons, is never allowed to be assuaged except by repentance and expiation. Deeply and irretrievably caught in the web of their passions, Deledda's characters sense that fate prevents them from fulfilling even their most modest dream. In turn, their disappointment becomes a kind of pervasive disenchantment with their lot. Suppressing their feelings, on the other hand, even when by prevailing standards they may be considered amoral or immoral, is hardly a satisfactory solution, for much wretchedness ensues. There is neither an end nor a final answer to such an unbearable, vicious cycle.

This particular point is effectively dramatized by Deledda in *Elias Portulu* (1903). The novel presents the predicament of a man who, after having been unjustly jailed for a crime he has not committed, returns to his home in Sardinia, anxious to live a decent and honest life. He falls in love with Maddalena Scade, who is betrothed to his brother Pietro. Maddalena returns his love; yet social traditions are such that the two will never be able to marry. Their uncontrollable passion in the context of an inflexible social context can only lead to a sinful love affair. In order to avoid further temptations, Elias decides to enter a seminary and become a priest. His decision is only partly motivated by a call to a religious life: we sense that it is but a way to avoid a conflict with his brother by declaring his feelings and thus prevent the marriage from taking place, as his shepherd friend, Martinu Monne has advised him to do. Maddalena and Pietro are thus united in holy matrimony, but their marriage proves to be a larger disaster than anyone could have anticipated. Maddalena becomes increasingly more restless and unhappy, maltreated by her vulgar husband who proves to be a violent drunkard unable to provide for his family. The story takes a sudden turn when Pietro quite unexpectedly dies. Elias, who is yet to be ordained, could elect to follow an ancient custom that permits marrying his brother's wife so as to care for the family of the deceased. Instead, lacking the strength to abandon the priesthood, afraid that his marriage may be misinterpreted, he lets Maddalena marry Jacopo Farre, a wealthy farmer. Elias's feelings are now more confused than ever: he detests the man who has taken his place next to a woman he loves and who now tries to be a good father to Elias's own son Berte; at the same time, he feels guilty of the unworthy manner in which he serves his Lord. Shortly after his birth, Berte falls ill and, despite the tender care of his mother and stepfather, dies. Elias Portulu prepares the little body for burial and realizes how close he has always been to him and how he could have been a good father had he only decided to follow the dictates of his instinct. The pattern already present in Deledda's first book, aptly titled *La via del male* [The path of evil] is repeated once more: man moves from innocence to guilt and then—through his awareness of past sins—to expiation. Events and circumstances change, to be sure, but the pattern keeps on repeating itself here and elsewhere in Deledda's stark novels.

La via del male and *Elias Portulu* give an intimation of Deledda's view of life. Man's lot is far from being a happy one. Much like the events of a fable narrated by a servant to the writer in her girlhood, they form sad segments of a journey when the questions are many and the answers are few. The fable, as Deledda relates in the autobiographical book *Cosima*, made "a profound, almost physical impression; the mystery of the fable, the final silence, the eternal story of [man's] error, punishment, sorrow." "[Human] destiny, death, man" who is himself nothing but ashes (and *Ashes* is the apt title of another of her novels); "fate is like the wind," she remarks in *Canne al vento*). What does man understand of the reasons for living, suffering, dying? Is he not doomed to eternal ignorance, a slave of an unknown Master, always buffeted by his many tormenting passions only to be haunted by spiritual remorse?

These are the chief questions posed, but never directly answered, in the narrative of Grazia Deledda. The Sardinian prefers to present her heroes and heroines suffering, pursued by temptations, thrown into perplexing situations, groping in their quest for the answer to their dilemmas. Perhaps such is man's greatest punishment.

The story of man's original sin, of God's subsequent wrath, and of man's sense of loss in a universe that makes little sense to him is repeated again and again by Deledda's characters. They are frequently easy preys of their sensual instincts, persecuted by conventions they cannot overcome.

Even an honest repentance proves to be insufficient to restore their peace of mind. It is difficult, however, to resist temptations, for man is by nature weak and his flesh is willing. Traditions, social customs, nature itself seem almost to become enjoined in a conspiracy to make the human dream of happiness on earth but a dim mirage. Life is toil, deprivation, sorrow, restlessness.

Canne al vento is yet another handling of the familiar theme of crime and punishment. It tells the story of Efix, now an old man and the faithful servant of three aging sisters, Ruth, Esther, and Noemi Pintor, who have lost their modest possessions and are forced to live a retiring, semi-destitute existence. Efix's conscience troubles him constantly, for he feels the remorse of a crime unintentionally committed in his younger days. Several years earlier, while helping the older Pintor sister, Lia (with whom he was secretly in love), escape to the mainland to a happier, freer existence, Efix accidentally killed her father, don Zame, who was trying to prevent her from leaving home. Since that time much has happened. Lia married, had a child, and has passed away. Now her son Giacinto has come home to Sardinia and to his family, not because he is lonely but, as we soon discover, because it is impossible for him to get a job on the mainland. His record has been stained by a theft he has perpetrated while working for the customs authorities.

Once back home, he proves to be a weak man; obsessed by his vice of gambling, he contracts numerous debts, drives his aunts to total bankruptcy, forcing them to sell their sole remaining property, a small farm, to their cousin don Predu. Efix's situation becomes all the more painful when he learns that Giacinto is acquainted with his crime: haunted by his past, wishing to repent for a murder he has committed, and driven by a strong desire to help the three ladies whose servant he is, he gives himself to begging in the streets. Only a marriage between Noemi and don Predu could save the household, but the proud girl stubbornly refuses to consider the possibility. Efix's sense of duty calls him back to the Pintor household, where he feels his presence is needed now that one of the sisters, Ruth, has died. At this point the story takes a turn for the better: Noemi agrees to marry don Predu, while Giacinto mends his ways, finds a job, and plans to marry Griselda, a young girl whom he has met on the island. Efix can die peacefully now: old, tired, and almost totally blind, he perceives that although he has not discovered the reasons for his anguish, he can at least attempt to offer his own synthesis of the human condition with the very words that give the book its apt title: "We are," he notes sadly as he is dying, "but reefs at the mercy of the wind!" "Fate," he concludes, "is like the wind." What Efix is in effect implying is that man by his very finite, imperfect nature is excluded from a real knowledge of the inner reasons of his suffering, feeling like a pilgrim at home nowhere, incessantly traveling toward an unknown destination. Indeed, in this respect it is significant that Deledda uses a servant as one of the central figures of her books. Man, we might deduct, is but a servant of his Lord. Like the servant of Deledda's fiction, he must be faithful, silent, obedient, enduring. He must be the executor of a superior Will and never aspire to a change in his condition of servitude: to change it would mean to shatter the social, moral, and religious order that gives the world its special meaning.

Deledda's heroes are perennially under the spell of destiny. If they are uneducated this should not be construed to mean that they are insensitive. It does mean that ultimately they are able to view their predicament only emotionally. They can neither intellectualize their experience nor draw from it significant norms of conduct. It has been said that their crises take place in their conscience: in the dramatic confrontation between good and evil that forms the very core of their drama, they find themselves at once unwilling participants and spectators, suspecting but never certain that their dilemma has neither an end, except in death, nor a solution, except in resignation. Whatever happens to them seems preordained by a superior force, and there is little indeed they can do to change what seems an inevitable course of events. They sense the presence of the demon in the air about themselves, but are unable to detect it clearly. "What is the demon?" asks Uncle Martinu in *Elias Portulu*.

The cryptic answer has a Sartrian flavor: "The demon is our-selves."

It is an unavoidable factor of man's condition that he is condemned to experience pain. There cannot be real joy in life for him, unless he has first undergone the trial of suffering: man can hardly be ready for salvation unless he first experiences evil and learns to reject it. We know but little about life and ourselves, Martinu points out in *Elias Portulu*, until we have felt the touch of pain, the anguish of having to break a rule or a law, or to hate, betray, until we know what it is to persecute or to be persecuted. Evil, in one form or another, is ever-present in life: in the world of Deledda, man is engaged in a fierce battle to combat it, for it must be destroyed not just once but every single day of our lives.

Evil is indeed the element most directly responsible for the predicament in which Deledda's heroes find themselves. If this is an obvious fact to the attentive reader, it is less easy to define just what is the nature of such evil. An exhaustive reading of Deledda's novels sheds precious little light upon this question. In fact, rather than expanding her original definition of evil as something inherent to man, Deledda contents herself with pointing out its variety and complexity. To be sure, there is a definite Verghian coloring to the substance of her tales. Unlike Verga, whose characters are doomed to be vanquished despite the small victories they secure in their struggle "to improve their economic lot," Deledda is more intent in showing us the human incapacity of understanding life, the futility of combating the rigid social and religious structure in which her characters live. At times, evil springs unexpectedly from an act certainly not intended to break an existing order. In *Canne al vento*, for example, the tragedy that soon overtakes many lives is directly traceable to Efix's bold glances at his mistress Lia, who eventually abandons her native town in Sardinia for the mainland, where she hopes to find love and happiness. Both characters have broken an established order; and both will pay the consequences of their act. Similarly, Elias Portulu violates God's law by wanting his brother's betrothed, then simply aggravates the situation by deciding not to marry the girl, even though circumstances have changed and his brother's death makes their union possible. After having failed to seize his last opportunity to be happy, he lives the balance of his life regretting his decision.

For Deledda, life is a source of continuous temptations that are hard to avoid. Only an iron will or total resignation to a feudal condition succeeds in resisting the opportunities life holds out to man. In *La via del male* [The path of evil], (1896; revised 1906), for a long time the protagonist Maria avoids a direct involvement with her servant Pietro Benu, who loves her deeply and, despite his inferior social condition, hopes that his love will be returned. The power of conventions is too strong, and Maria marries a moderately wealthy landowner, Francesco Rosana, while Pietro, unjustly accused of participating in the theft of some sheep, is jailed. When he is released several weeks later he decides to revenge himself, becomes a professional thief and amasses a small fortune in a short time. One day, Francesco is found murdered; five years later Maria accepts Pietro's request to marry him. A few days later, she receives a letter from Sabina, a woman obviously in love with Pietro. The letter reveals that Francesco was actually murdered by Maria's second husband. The two are now condemned to a special kind of punishment, for they will live together as man and wife with a haunting awareness of the individual role they have played in a crime that has killed a man and ruined another. Thus, Deledda's characters live perennially torn between resigning themselves to a condition that will not bring them happiness, or violating certain social codes, in full knowledge that their actions will inevitably disturb the precarious balance of an order presumably capable of bringing about both peace and happiness.

It would be futile, in the last analysis, to insist on demanding of Deledda a coherent, rationally expressed vision of life, a statement that through images and events might explain the human condition. As some critics have perceived, her fiction exists not to expound a well-defined social or moral ideology, but in order to re-create a mood, a feeling,

an atmosphere. In the vagueness of her tales resides much of
her charm as well as her limitations as a writer; in the in-
definiteness of the psychology of her characters is their authenticity as people. Deledda's heroes do what they do—
love, suffer, resign themselves to stifling conventions,
commit acts of violence, and live a life haunted by tragic
memories—simply because this is the lot of a human being's
conscience to bear. Perhaps the answer to why life must be
so is to be found in the final pages of Deledda's early novel,
La via del male. Maria has just learned that her husband is
the killer of her first mate. Whereupon the author comments: "She was born to fight, to struggle, to stab people in
their back. She has always betrayed. She betrayed Pietro, her
relatives, Sabina. She has betrayed even Francesco by not
confessing the truth to him. Perhaps he would not have died
had she spoken. But the world is full of betrayals and deceits: man must fight against man so as to have his share of
sun and earth."

Marino Moretti

If you should ever have the chance to visit Cesenatico, the colorful fishing and summer resort town on the
Adriatic coast, in the Romagna region, cross the bridge over
the canal dividing the town, turn right, and on your left
you will find the house of Marino Moretti. Everyone in
town seems to know and esteem its most illustrious citizen
who has done so much to make the Romagna famous by
fictionalizing it in his work—"a Romagna," as Giuseppe
Ravegnani felicitously remarked, "peopled by common characters. . . . tied to the humble reality of their occupation,
to the scheme of time and feelings." Moretti, poet and
novelist, is of course more than a good writer: he is a
minor artist who has given a special dimension to his native
place, transforming it into a kind of stage in miniature
where the men and women he has observed from his window and in the streets reenact the universal drama of living.
It was in Cesenatico that Moretti was born on July 18,
1885, and it was there that he received his first education

from his mother, a certified elementary school teacher whose influence on his intellectual and spiritual development proved to be fundamental. If Marino was a good scholar as a child, he certainly was not as he progressed into high school, first in nearby Ravenna and later on in Bologna. His disappointing academic performance and his diminishing interest in classical studies led to his decision to enroll in the Drama Academy in Florence, at that time the cultural capital of the nation. There he struck a friendship with people who, like Aldo Palazzeschi, were to become the leading writers and critics of his generation. It was also in Florence that Moretti observed close at hand and profited from the work of deprovincialization of Italian culture being carried out by the various reviews that were springing up one after the other at the turn of the century.

Barely twenty, Moretti decided to make writing his life's career. His first poems began appearing in several magazines, and, in 1905 his first collection of lyrics appeared with the significant title *Fraternità* [Brotherhood]. In the same year, he published a collection of his short stories humorously titled *Il paese degli equivoci* [The town of misunderstandings]. Moretti's job, as assistant to the editor of a dictionary of Italian actors apparently did not slow down his creative activity: volumes of poetry continued to appear: *La Serenata delle zanzare* [The seranade of mosquitoes] in 1908; *Poesie scritte col lapis* [Poems written with a pencil] in 1910; *Poesie di tutti i giorni* [Everyday poems] in 1911; *I Poemetti di Marino* [Marino's short poems] in 1913, as well as semiautobiographical books, *I Lestofanti* [The nimble ones] (1909); *Ah, ah, ah!* in 1910. And such was the beginning of one of the most prolific of contemporary Italian writers.

Moretti's first important break came in 1910, when an urbane young critic of the European literary scene, Giuseppe A. Borgese, reviewed the state of recent Italian poetry in the September 10 issue of the respected Turinese newspaper *La Stampa*. Borgese's article is still valuable not merely for its sensitive, if on the whole negative, assessment of the work of three young poets, Moretti, Martini, and Chiaves,

but for the term *Crepuscolare* ("twilight") he coined to
describe such poetry. "What Italian poetry is, after the
glorious flowering of Pascoli and d'Annunzio," he wrote, "is
not easy to understand for someone who has no professional
interest in literature. . . . If one asks the mass audience,
one would say . . . that after the *Laudi* and the *Poemetti*,
Italian poetry has become extinguished. It has faded away,
to be sure, but in a mild and very long twilight, which perhaps will not be followed by the [darkness of] night."
Borgese's comments are less restrained in the body of his
article, particularly when evaluating the collection of lyrics
by Moretti, *Poems written with a Pencil*, which he defined
"pale stuff, bloodless, cold . . ." "The poet," he added,
"knows his malaise, but does not take care of it, as though
taking care of it should turn the subject matter of his poetry
into dust in his own hands."

It was inevitable that, after the dash and brilliance of the
so-called Triad of Italian poetry—Carducci, Pascoli, and
d'Annunzio—the young generation of writers should feel
confused regarding their direction, particularly those who
felt they did not have much in common with their predecessors. The "Poetry of the Twilight" with all its obvious
limitations, eventually proved to be more than a "sluggish
and muddy melancholy of having nothing to say and nothing to do." The new poetry not only rejected the glorious,
patriotic, and bombastic themes of the past *maestri*, it committed itself to reduce the high level of rhetoric spreading
like a malignant cancer through the body of much of Italian
literature. Their inspiration was very modest, to be sure:
Sunday promenades, days spent at home watching the rain
falling, morbid visits to hospital dormitories, the boredom
of provincial life. The eyes were trained on the past, for the
present was, as is often the case, unbearable to contemplate.

> *Piove. E' mercoledí. Sono a Cesena*
> *ospite della ma sorella sposa,*
> *sposa da sei, da sette mesi appena . . .*
>   ("A Cesena")

["It's raining. It's Wednesday, I am at Cesena / guest of

my   married   sister / married   for   six,   barely   seven
months . . ."]   [At Cesena]

The *Crepuscolari* did not have a special program; yet,
through their poetry, they clearly indicated their intention
to avoid both the classics of Carducci and the verbal pyro-
technics of d'Annunzio. Stylistically and thematically, they
had much in common with Pascoli who, in theory and
practice, had demonstrated the potentials of a language
which, in its simplicity and naïveté, imitated the elementary
expressiveness of a child discovering for the first time the
mystery of nature and the wonderment of life.

The lesson of the "Twilight" experience proved to be particularly important for Moretti not so much for the im-
mediate results it yielded, but for the general direction in
which he moved as a novelist. His art was deeply rooted in
the simple, religious yet sensual Romagna region where he
was born, while his quality as a visionary man of letters was
shaped by his strong desire to see life clearly and directly,
even at the cost of oversimplifying complex issues. In this
sense, the term *Crepuscolare* (one Moretti undoubtedly
would reject even if used for the understandable purpose of
"historicizing" his literary production), acquires in his work
a positive value in that it pinpoints both the strength and
the weakness of his fiction. He is at his best when he describes in an unusually honest manner humble folk who
lead an ordinary existence—their trepidations, expectations,
and hopes. Moretti knows such people well; he understands
their way of looking at the world, a way deeply rooted in
their simple beginnings. And because he is particularly
aware of the melancholy character of their lives, he manages to be particularly effective when he concentrates on the
sadness of their condition. His temperament is such that he
seldom resorts to using violent colors. The evening is preferred to the day, for it brings the opportunity to meditate
and pray, and forces us to reexamine our personal conduct
and the nature of our predicament, making us particularly
aware of the loneliness and the quiet despair of life. We
find ample evidence of this in Moretti's early poetry and we

find it developed and enriched in his short stories and novels.

Moretti's links with his native literary traditions are unmistakable: like Manzoni, he is essentially a Catholic writer; like Manzoni and Verga, he focuses primarily, if not exclusively, upon the world of the poor and the disinherited. At times, his characters have something in common with Pascoli's *fanciullino* ("little child"). Indeed, it is here that we begin seeing the emergence of the human being who discovers the beauty and magic of nature but is soon struck down by its violence. Life, first envisioned as exciting and full of surprises, now appears in all its cruelty. There are conflicts, disappointments, and frustrations. And there is the ultimate realization of the frailty of human existence. Life may seem to promise much, but delivers little. The struggle for survival is both long and constant, and suffering is one of life's most constant ingredients. "Here is [Moretti's] sentimental, deformed world," the critic Luigi Russo once remarked, "young, mischievous students who skip school and become bored, old men teachers and spinster teachers, young ladies who are neither beautiful nor ugly, and stray dogs, poor people without help, unmarried people without love, mediocre adventures, boring Sundays, creatures and things, in fine, all allowed to live and who do live, a feminine world par excellence, pale and emaciated." One of the titles of Moretti's books succeeds in catching the condition of his characters: *Pesci fuor d'acqua* [Fishes out of water] (1914), doomed to live in an alien milieu, painfully aware of their condition. And with this book, as Francesco Casnati notes, Moretti begins describing not his little world of personal memories, nostalgias, and feelings, but the "world of the others," "with a clairvoyance that is between compassion and irony, a sense of life [that is] serious and gray, a judgment of people and things already firm and circumscribed, in the resigned persuasion of universal mediocrity and inevitable evil." The world now is presented as a strange place where man is but a pilgrim in a never-ending quest for knowledge and fulfillment while preparing himself for the eternal life after death. Life tests our world:

living, however important it may seem to us, is really incidental to the eternity of life beyond our own.

For Moretti, 1911 marked an eventful year: he took the
manuscript of his first novel to the prestigious publishing
firm of Emilio Treves, only to be flatly turned down. The
young man persevered: his next referee was a man with
some influence, Goffredo Bellonci, at that time coeditor
with Emilio Cecchi of the cultural page of the daily *Gior-
nale d'Italia*. This time the verdict was favorable. The novel
was accepted, and appeared first in serialized form and a
few years later in book form with the Treves imprint.

The book's title, *Il sole del sabato* [The sun of the sab-
bath] (1916), is after an old adage, "There is no Saturday
without sun, there is no woman without love." Much like
the titles of his poems and other prose works (which include literary vignettes, short stories, and a score of autobiographical books), there is much irony in the title. The
heroine of the story is Barberina, the common ancestor of a
long gallery of women created by Moretti's fertile imagination. Like any other woman, she yearns for love, for fulfillment as a wife and as a mother. She has an affair with two
men, Mauro and Niblin, and is married by the former. She
gives birth to a child, but Mauro immediately disclaims his
paternity. Abandoned by her husband, she is haunted by
Niblin who asserts that the child is his, and so should be
the woman who gave her birth. The child falls ill and dies.
Life holds nothing more for Barberina: as the book ends, we
follow her going back to her birthplace, the malaria-
infested *valle*, and to her mother, herself abandoned by her
husband.

Il sole del sabato is a static book, moving less horizontally
than vertically. One might say that ultimately it tells less
the story of the unhappy events of a woman than the way
she conquers humility, resignation, patience as she goes
through a series of disasters. Indeed, the women of Moretti
find their strength through their unhappiness, for they accept everything that happens to them as manifestation of
God's Will, and see in the way they cope with their setbacks
a clear test of their faith in the Lord. The situations change,

but the characters walk the same Calvary. Their names are not the same (after Barberina there is Cristina, Clarice, Gianna, Mimma, and so on), but their experiences and fate differ only in matters of details. No one has the right to rebel against God's Will: we must accept what is meted out to us, and remember the teachings of our Lord, whose Gospel, together with *The Imitation of Christ,* is quoted again and again. There is Barberina going "home," who is reminded that "there is no greater servant than his Master. If they persecute Me, they will persecute you. . . ." and there is Menghinina, of *La voce di Dio* [The voice of the Lord] (1920). Menghinina is the humble servant of Cristina, a young woman who returns home after several years spent in the city, at times symbolic of corruption and temptation. Since in small Italian towns being a *signora*—i.e., a married woman—is an accepted sign of social status, Cristina tells friends and acquaintances that she is married. She soon falls prey of her sensuality, has an affair with a married man, and is crushed by her experience. Her child must lose his life before birth, so that she may live. Here Menghinina does not follow strictly the way of her peers and predecessors: at the end of the book, she blows out the light always lit in front of the picture of the Virgin Mary in what must be considered an inconsistent and unjustified act of revolt against the "voice of God" she has always listened to in her life.

The two women, in more than one way, reflect two sharply divided views of life Moretti holds out: Cristina struggles to find happiness and fulfillment, and for her neither can be achieved except in and through her sensuality; Menghinina, on the other hand, accepts the more orthodox view that happiness and love mean being devoted to our Maker, respecting the home (and here Moretti is preciously near Verga), accepting the centuries-old traditions that have served her ancestors in good stead, loving her neighbors, having compassion for all men, and understanding the finite quality of human life. The extreme diversity of these views of life are basic in the world of Moretti, and indeed they also constitute the element of tension in his work. It is no mere accident that the drama of this conflict is frequently emphasized by the strategic choice of the locale where Moretti's stories unfold: the Romagna, a region with a long tradition of violence and sensuality, the land that gave birth to Mussolini and has long been a breeding ground for radical political parties, socialism, communism and fascism. The conflict between strength and weakness, pride and humility, between sensual love and Christian love is found time and again: Fortunata Saladini, the protagonist of *I puri di cuore* [The pure of heart] (1923), is a proud, selfish woman who sees two of her children, Alma and Matteo, defeated by life while her partly mentally retarded son Luca, a shining example of humility, manages to survive and conquer the respect and affection of his mother, inspiring in everyone with whom he comes into contact compassion for their neighbors. There is Marino Fogliani, of *Il trono dei poveri*, [The throne of the poor] (1928), citizen of the Republic of San Marino whose smallness and poverty determine both the quality of its life and the character of its people. Marino, an aspiring playwright, leaves his town and goes to Rome where he meets Viviana Montalbo, a woman he had first known in San Marino, falls in love with her daughter Ape, and ends being Viviana's lover. At the outbreak of World War I, Viviana's children, Ape and Oscar, volunteer their services as does Marino, who accepts a lowly assignment in the Red Cross as a hospital orderly. Months later, Marino and Viviana meet again in the hospital: Oscar is dead now, and the two realize the impossibility of resuming their former relation. He returns home to marry a childhood sweetheart and is elected Regent of the Republic for the customary term of six months. No one better than Marino's former teacher, Ser Menetto di Menetto di Bonelli, articulates the fundamental teaching, the lasting lesson, as it were, of the Republic of San Marino. "I should like to recommend parsimony to you. . . . Without [our] weakness we could not have saved ourselves; without parsimony we could not have maintained ourselves weak and disarmed . . . San Marino's freedom [alone] is still not enough: we must conquer liberty of God's children, the liberation of the humble, of the pure, of the poor, of all those who on this earth search first of all God's Kingdom and his Justice. . . ."

Year after year, Marino Moretti has written with delicacy, humor, and imagination about the *Romagnoli*: the fishermen, the laborers, the peasants, the priests, but above all, the women. The gallery of characters he has created is large and impressive: they are people who are struck time and again by small and large misfortunes, who love, who are capable of suffering without being driven to despair. There is something both admirable and reassuring about their capacity to endure their disappointments and disasters —a capacity one might be tempted to call heroic, were it not for the fact that their intense religiosity prevents them from understanding, let alone accepting the fundamentally tragic nature of the human condition.

Moretti's portraiture of women is of the highest quality, particularly when they are peasants or lowly working people: they are humble and tough, and yet they are moved by compassion; they understand life far better than the menfolk and their understanding has been gained not only through their experience, but through having endured many indignities because of their social status and sex. Their wisdom, if one can generalize about this aspect, is a mixture of religiousness, strength, common sense, and resignation. Not all of Moretti's women are "good," to be sure. But even when they lack what we call moral qualities, they show an unexpected capacity to handle their problems with considerable confidence. Moretti's male characters, on the other hand, include a fair share of speculators, manipulators, and deceivers. They are often rough and even violently sensual, frequently responsible for corrupting the moral world they inhabit. In this respect, they balance the inner goodness and simplicity of their female counterparts. One must bear in mind that Moretti painstakingly depicts a world that has now almost completely vanished from today's scene, the rural or provincial town with its special mores, its God-fearing people, peasants, servants. In every way his milieu is realistically described, accurate both in its details and its psychology. Where Moretti does, to some extent, fail is in the presentation of ethically strong male characters, an inadequacy that may be traceable to the absence in his own life of a father figure. Surprisingly enough, even in his autobiographical books there is hardly a reference to his father. In *Via Laura* (originally subtitled *The Book of My Surprising Twenty Years*) Moretti tells us of his decision not to continue his academic studies. His mother seems to have immediately understood and accepted his decision, and, rather than showing her disappointment, supported him, while his father, obviously an old-fashioned individual, "as always, heard [me] and yet did not understand."

Structurally and stylistically, Moretti's novels, for all their undeniable qualities, are conventional. His range is limited but his perspective is clear and uncompromising. He has something in common with Manzoni's deeply felt religiousness and with Verga's ability to present convincingly the life of the poor. Unlike the great Sicilian master who fashioned a new language through which he found a new dimension for his characters, Moretti writes in a fluid, literary Italian, free from the pretentiousness and extreme concern with the preciousness and the niceties of the written language. To be sure, when occasion demands, much like Fogazzaro he exploits terms, expressions, or songs, as well as riddles of his native Romagna, to add to the authenticity of the scene. His knowledge of folklore is both vast and accurate; expertly used as it is in many of Moretti's books, it contributes much to their color. Yet, some of the elements we have thus far discussed contribute to his weaknesses as a novelist. "Moretti," writes Emilio Cecchi, "does not have great qualities of composition. He conceives the novel, or the short story, as an almost declining development of a theme to which it is sufficient to add [an] indispensable vividness and chiaroscuro—and not as an architecture of opposing forces." This may be why, from their very beginning, Moretti's novels deal with characters facing a situation where the odds are clearly stacked against them, where there is hardly a possibility of breaking out of the circle of unhappiness and sadness. Delicate and sensitive as Moretti's novels frequently are, they hold few surprises for the reader. Written almost invariably within the framework of Christian ideology, where "peace" can be attained only by accepting the only uncontroversial truth there is—the truth of God's Word revealed to us through the Bible and the Gospel—Moretti's novels lack the fire and deep intellectual commitment of, say, Claudel and Bernanos. In their own modest ways, however, Moretti's novels are effective (particularly those composed before the 1940s) in giving us a sense of the raw passions of man: his hunger for sensual love, his violent instincts, his awareness of the frailties of human beings. Although no critic would assign him a prominent position among modern novelists, there is much what he has written that commends him to our attention: the gentleness of spirit, the genuine humility of the characters he has created in so many of his books, the quality of his style—restrained, modest and frequently intensely poetic—are the pervasive characteristics of much of what he has composed in a life rich with achievements and serious writing. Moretti, as such a severe critic as Luigi Russo summed it up in his *I Narratori*, "has given us significant pages in the midst of the confused production of contemporary novels."

8

Luigi Pirandello: Man and his Masks

"Nous sommes si accoutumés à nous déguiser aux autres qu'enfin nous nous déguisons à nous-mêmes."

La Rochefoucauld

"An *oeuvre*," George Steiner remarked some years ago, implies a logic of unfolding, of gradually revealed design." This is unquestionably what separates a mere writer, however talented, who is interested in the limited objective of producing a well-developed, interesting narrative, from a literary artist, for whom every line of what he creates must by necessity serve his ultimate function, one I would call that of being an architect of the soul. The artist strives "to achieve continuity, to make individual acts of creation part of a natural growth and completion."

In the history of modern Italian letters, and indeed of modern world literature, Pirandello stands out as a giant, not merely for his astonishing insights into the human predicament, but for the sheer quality and quantity of his opus: seven long novels, two hundred and thirty-three short stories, over forty plays, and a thick volume of poetry and essays. Few writers in modern times have received as much attention as he did, and fewer still have produced a body of work that has been subject of wild praise and slanderous attacks by the critics, readers, and audiences. The controversial, yet seminal nature of his *oeuvre* is reflected in the term *Pirandellian* or *Pirandellism,* which much like *Proustian* or

Kafkaesque have been coined to define the unique manner in which later artists looked upon reality, inventing new techniques or styles to present their interpretations of the human condition.

That an artist's vision is frequently the result of his private life is, to a larger degree than usual, true in Pirandello's case. He was born at Càos, near the ancient town of Girgenti (now Agrigentum), located in the southeastern part of Sicily, on June 28, 1867, the year of a cholera epidemic that claimed over fifty thousand lives. "Born," as his official biographer Federico V. Nardelli writes, "on the edge of a calamity. Suddenly. And without a midwife." Being born in Sicily in the post-*Risorgimento* period was something bound to have a strong, if subtle, influence on the sensitivity of young Luigi, as we shall see. A great deal of what he wrote reflects the quality as well as the conflicts of a civilization largely shaped by Arab and Greek culture: "Essentially," Olga Ragusa notes in her essay on Pirandello, "the Arabic heritage meant a rigidly formal and immobile social structure, with its accompanying sense of reticence and secretiveness, its private language full of allusions instead of open statements, and the blocking of the individual's psyche, with the perennial danger of a sudden and irremediable explosion."

Pirandello's family was comfortably middle-class, economically and politically liberal. His father, Stefano, who had served with Garibaldi in 1860 and 1862, derived his livelihood from his interests in a sulphur mine, and hoped his son would follow in his footsteps. Luigi had other plans, however. He enrolled at the Law School of the University of Palermo, only to change his mind and transfer to the University of Rome in 1887. Soon after, he moved to the Faculty of Letters and Philosophy as he began thinking of a writing and teaching career. An argument with one of his teachers resulted in his expulsion from the University. After a summer visit to Girgenti, on the advice of Professor Ernesto Monaci Pirandello went to Bonn, where he studied under the direction of a renowned philologist, Wendelin Foerster. In 1891, after completing his dissertation on the dialect of his native Girgenti, Luigi returned to Italy and settled in Rome. There, thanks to a modest allowance from his father, he managed to live a comfortable, if unpretentious existence. At that time Rome was fast becoming the intellectual capital of the nation, and Pirandello was introduced to many of the influential writers, journalists, and critics. One of them, Luigi Capuana, the theoretical *caposcuola* of *verismo*, read Luigi's work and encouraged him to abandon poetry, which he had been writing since his adolescent years, for fiction—an advice that was to prove its importance only decades later.

In 1894, acceding to his father's desires, Luigi married Antonietta Portulano, daughter of his father's senior partner. It was a marriage "arranged" and not without its share of happy moments. Three years later, now father of three sons, realizing that it was extremely difficult for a writer to earn his livelihood from his art, Pirandello accepted a post at the Normal School in Rome. In 1903, disaster struck like lightning: Pirandello's father, prone to speculative ventures, having lost everything he had, including Antonietta's dowry which he had held in trust, was forced to file for bankruptcy. The effects were twofold: Luigi would no longer receive financial help from his father and Antonietta, who had already given signs of psychic instability, suffered a severe nervous breakdown. The consequences of her illness were serious indeed, and plagued her until her death in 1959. From 1903 until 1919, when she was finally placed in a special asylum, Pirandello insisted in keeping his wife home, even though her paranoic fits of jealousy made his life and their children's unbearable.

The steady deterioration of Antonietta's health and his own uncertain financial situation forced Pirandello to turn to writing as a source of income rather than the self-fulfilling activity it had been. According to Gaspare Giudice, Pirandello's recent biographer, royalties and fees more than doubled his professorial stipend of roughly 2,500 lire. *Il fu Mattia Pascal* (1904; *The Late Mattia Pascal*, N.Y., 1964), one of Pirandello's best-known and most successful novels, was commissioned by *La Nuova Antologia* and was written at his wife's bedside to earn money desperately needed to meet his growing obligations.

In 1908, his critical and creative work won Pirandello the chair of Italian Language and Literature at the Normal School, a post he relinquished in 1922 to devote his full attention to writing, directing, and producing his own plays. The *succes de scandale* achieved by his *Sei personaggi in cerca d'autore* (1921; *Six Characters in Search of an Author*, N.Y., 1952) thrust his name in the avant-garde of European writers. The situation was not without its special irony, when we realize that by that time he had already produced two volumes of essays, some fifteen different collections of short stories, dozens of one- and three-act plays, all but his last novel, *Uno, nessuno e centomila* (1926; *One, None and a Hundred Thousand*, N.Y., 1933). Another writer might have reacted ecstatically to the increasing attention he was receiving. Not Pirandello. Success never went to his head. He was fundamentally a reserved person who, although irked by adverse critical notices, seldom indulged in polemics, the most famous of such exceptions being the confrontation with Benedetto Croce who had coldly dismissed Pirandello's work on the doubtful proposition of its philosophical confusion and had savagely attacked his essay "On Humor." In his personal life Pirandello preferred anonymity to flamboyance, content to live in modest hotel rooms when he traveled with his repertory company. Only twice did he accept any honors: in 1929 when he was made a member of the newly reconstituted Accademia d'Italia, and in 1934 when he traveled to Sweden to accept the Nobel Prize for literature. His involvement in national politics was limited, even though his record does have its share of inconsistencies. In 1923 he joined the Fascist party, supporting its aggressive colonial policies (as in the case of the invasion of Ethiopia in 1935). Two years later he turned to Mussolini for financial support of one of his pet projects, the Teatro d'Arte di Roma. On the other hand, in 1927 he rebelled against the stupidities and pettiness of fascism by tearing up his party card. Later on he confessed: "I am apolitical: I consider myself to be only a man on earth . . ."

He died in 1936. His instructions contained in his last will and testament offer still other indications of the kind of Spartan simplicity he cherished. He requested that his body be cremated, "but, if this cannot be done," he continued, "let my funeral urn be taken to Sicily and be walled up in some rough country stone of Girgenti, where I was born." A quarter of a century after his death, his fiction and his plays continue to speak eloquently to men everywhere.

Pirandello's early work, consisting of poems, short stories, and plays, shows at once his links with the traditions of *verismo* and naturalism into which he was born, and his gradual disenchantment with their poetics. Regional settings, objectivity of treatment, stylistic simplicity—these and other elements can be easily discerned in his early writings. Soon enough it became clear to him that he was, *in fondo*, not at all interested in depicting regional life as was fashionable in the 1880s and 1890s, nor was he concerned with the broad economic or historical themes that abound in the fiction of his contemporaries who, like Verga and Capuana, had made man's economic struggle for survival or his passions the central subjects of their work. Even his choice of Sicily as the milieu of much of what he was to write was made for different reasons. "Sicily is to Pirandello," Cambon perceptively notes, "what the South is to Faulkner, what Ireland is to Joyce: a hopeless case, a fierce love, and a hotbed of anachronistic dreamers." He chose Sicily not because he intended to comment on certain peculiar conditions of his native island but because the brooding temperament of his fellowmen was a necessary element of the special world to which he wished to give life. He wanted to move, in short, from reality to a metaphysics that would never slight the "facts" of reality, so that he could analyze the roots and meaning of man's solitude, his condition of estrangement, his being "out of tune," a "violin and double bass," constantly *malgré lui*, caught in the web of his contradictions. And if there is a noticeable insistence of a relatively few themes, and if he insisted in addressing himself as a writer and as a critic to those problems that haunted his imagination, this was not to focus on "other" truths but, as the late contemporary novelist as Elio Vittorini might have said, to understand and illuminate more completely for himself and his readers his special truth. In this sense, he has less in common with most of his contemporaries who had been his first models than with such an "outsider" as Italo Svevo. Both focused on the internal condition of their characters, little concerned with action, suspense, plot development—in short, with the ingredients of the well-made novel. Both Svevo and Pirandello, despite their bourgeois background, are children of a particularly difficult era, the post-*Risorgimento* years with their mediocrity and hypocrisy. Writing in a period of great changes that saw the collapse of those values society had accepted as part and parcel of its cultural heritage, they recognized the impelling necessity to put aside some of the widely held assumptions about man and his interaction with society, and reinvestigate the entire concept of reality and the human personality. Thus, they became the challengers of accepted *modi vivendi*, searching for the factors that keep the insane sane while pointing out to those who are sane the general insanity of life. For Pirandello, the delicate mechanism of human behavior may be understood through a delicate fragmentization of what we call reality, and such a process permits us to come to grips with what another contemporary novelist, the late Cesare Pavese, called "the business of living."

There is ample evidence that Pirandello did not find his big themes and his style suddenly: both were the result of a slow, painful but exciting search that saw him experimenting with translations from the German, and translation into standard Italian of plays he had originally composed in his native dialect. He moved cautiously at first and used traditional structures to give life to his world view. But as he matured, his vision became sharper and the form of his plays and novels bolder. By the early twenties, Adriano Tilgher, one of his best philosophical critics, provided Pirandello with the formula *Forma-Vita* (form vs. life) which the Sicilian espoused enthusiastically for a while, rejecting it with unusual anger later on. Unfortunately, space rules out a detailed examination of the various elements that became the ingredients of his vision. At least two important items may be presented here. In a letter written in 1886 to his sister Lina, Pirandello stated: "If one looks at life, it seems to be an enormous puppet show, without any logical connection or explanation." "What is important," he wrote in one of his earliest short stories, "is not to fly faster or slower, higher or lower, but to know why one flies." Taken together, such observations reveal much of Pirandello's skepticism toward man and life, as well as his determination to analyze seriously what he considered to be its central issues. His faith in reality, or what generally goes under that name, decreased as he grew older. Again and again he denied his links with naturalism. In an interview granted to Domenico Vittorini upon his arrival in New York, Pirandello stated: "I feel that I am at the opposite pole from naturalism. I have battered down faith in clumsy, tangible reality"—an observation whose uncanny accuracy is obvious even in some of his early short stories.

As Pirandello came into his own, his break with certain views he had inherited became sharper. The new ground on which he was treading was, to use De Castris's words, "that of a man who has acquired the responsibility of a new dimension, i.e., of a consciousness mirroring and dramatizing himself, forced as he was to experience personally the crisis henceforth" (*Storia di Pirandello*). This implied not only a new concept of fiction, but a new awareness of the kind of writer he chose to be. For an explicit statement on this question, one must turn to the preface of the 1925 edition of *Six Characters* in which he elaborated on certain ideas he had expressed in a slightly different form in the early years of our century:

> To me, it was never enough to present a man or a woman and what is special and characteristic about them simply for the pleasure of presenting them; to narrate a particular affair, lively or sad, simply for the pleasure of narrating it; to describe a landscape simply for the pleasure of describing it.

There are some writers (and not a few), who do feel this pleasure and satisfied, ask no more. They are, to speak more precisely, historical writers.

But there are others who, beyond such pleasure, feel a more profound spiritual need on whose account they admit only figures, affairs, landscapes which have been soaked, so to speak, in a particular sense of life and acquire from it a university value. These are, more precisely, philosophical writers.

I have the misfortune to belong to these last.

The critical pronouncements of a writer are almost always, and with some justification, I believe, received with great caution by critics mainly because they address themselves to problems that ought to be resolved by his finished work. Nevertheless, if we bear in mind the usefulness of the critical papers of, say, Dante, Tasso, and Leopardi, we have the obligation of weighing such materials on the basis of their relevance to a better understanding of a writer's work. In this sense, Pirandello's essays frequently offer valuable insights into his approach to the art of fiction as he conceived it. This is most definitely the case of his essay "On Humor," written in 1904 and published in 1908, during the years when he was working on and publishing *Il fu Mattia Pascal*. The lengthy essay contains the chief tenets of Pirandello's poetics, particularly what he called *"l'avvertimento del contrario"* ("the awareness of the incongruous") and *"il sentimento del contrario"* ("the feeling of the incongruous"). In Pirandello's fiction and theatre, humor is given an unusual interpretation and an original role, for it becomes both a stance and a tool that permit the artist to probe deeply and interpret not only what we poor mortals call *reality* (and what Pirandello prefers calling *appearances*) but is behind the façade of reality. In its first phase, humor depicts what we see; in its second phase humor analyzes with considerable sympathy the contradictions inherent in existence itself. True enough, the author's depiction of the state of his characters contains a small measure of humor in the conventional meaning of the term; but the purpose of humor is not to make us laugh, however mildly, but to make us *understand* the anguish of people. As we shall see, Pirandello analyzes life by following a process of constant decomposition: the rather unusual (if indeed not bizarre) situations of his work are successfully made alive by the special formlessness that characterizes the bulk of his literary production.

The difference between the "awareness" and the "sense" of the incongruous may be readily grasped by paraphrasing Pirandello's own illustrative example: we see an old woman, whose dyed hair and heavy make-up and dress are inappropriate for a person of her age. Her appearance makes us laugh, because we realize that she is the opposite of what we think an old and respectable woman should look like. This, for the novelist, is the first stage of the process that leads us to a deeper analysis of the situation. In fact, though we instinctly may laugh at the sight of such a woman, we also begin to think about her situation: we then begin feeling that perhaps in her mind, her make-up and bizarre way of dressing are meant to make her more attractive to her young husband, whose love and attention she is obviously afraid to lose. At this point, we become more directly involved in the pathos of her situation. Our sympathy is aroused: we finally perceive that her special situation has been created to construct a mask that will hide her deepest emotions and anxieties while at the same time protect her from additional suffering.

Whether Pirandello's position is or is not truly original is irrelevant at this point. What does matter is its effectiveness in terms of the results it yields. One of the great artists of the cinema of all times, Charlie Chaplin, based many of his films on much the same contrasts presented by Pirandello's essay just discussed. Chaplin, in fact, very frequently reaches his greatest effects precisely when the audience, who has heartily been laughing at his clownish behavior, begins to realize that under those funny clothes—the baggy trousers, the tight black coat, the cardboard shirt, the bowler hat, the umbrella, and the large, odd-shaped shoes—there is a tender, sensitive human being with yearnings, desperately looking for work, happiness, and a contact with other human beings. We identify with Chaplin's tramp because through his amusing antics he manages to communicate with us; we admire his perseverance, we feel tenderness toward his sadness, and we are in complete sympathy with his efforts to fight the system in order to survive and achieve authenticity. Circumstances, the order of things, the very nature of man make survival difficult, frequently possible only by compromises. We grow older only to discover that the act of living forces us all, to one extent or another, to entertain illusions, particularly about ourselves; through illusions we see not what we are, but what we would like to be: "We think, operate, live according to this fictitious and yet insincere interpretation of ourselves," as Pirandello wrote. Here is where humor begins playing its vital role, particularly in helping us to single out those illusions that lead people to believe that social conventions are inspired by genuinely humane feelings, when in fact they are nothing if not "considerations of self-interest in which morality is almost always sacrificed." The hypocrisy that is at the very heart of human action enables us to resolve, or at least attenuate the contradictions we confront every day. The greater our spiritual and intellectual weakness is, the more urgent the need to resort to some kind of deception if we are to make peace with society.

The harder the struggle for life and the more one's weakness is felt, the greater becomes the need for mutual deception. The simulation of force, honesty, sympathy, prudence, in short, of every virtue, and that greatest virtue veracity, is a form of adjustment, an effective instrument of struggle. . . .

While the sociologist describes social life as it presents itself to external observation, the humorist, being a man of exceptional intuition, shows—nay, reveals—that appearances are one thing and the consciousness of the people concerned, in its inner essence, another. And yet people "lie psychologically," even as they "lie socially." And this lying to ourselves—living, as we do, on the sur-

face and not in the depths of our being—is the result of
the social lying. The mind that gives back its own reflection is a solitary mind, but our internal solitude is never
so great that suggestions from the communal life do not
break upon it with all the fiction and transferences which
characterize them.

So wrote Pirandello in his pivotal essay "On Humor."
To be sure, Pirandello did not arrive at his particular views
of the world independently, and one may turn to several
studies for a more detailed analysis of his sources. Yet, by
raising questions of fundamental importance in the business
of living, he became one of the first writers to define fiction-
ally what later literary artists—Sartre, Camus, Ionescu, and
Beckett among others—called "the sense of the absurd."
"Camus," as Beatrice Corrigan notes, "defined the absurd
as 'the stranger who at certain seconds comes to meet us in
the mirror,'" and "in Pirandello's plays"—as well as in
much of his fiction, one might add—"it is always when a
man sees an unfamiliar image of himself in the mirror of
other people's opinions that his tragedy begins." The questions Pirandello asks in his short stories, in his novels, and
in his plays became, indeed, the leitmotifs of his work:
what must a sensitive person do to exist in peace with the
"others" in a society that systematically shows its unaware-
ness of the pain of living? How can the human race retain
its sanity in a world of contradictions, where scandalously
immoral judgments are an everyday occurence and where
corruption of values is rampant? How can man, condemned
a priori to a condition of isolation, an island unto himself,
communicate with his fellowmen? What are the possibilities and limitations of language?

Pirandello, writes Paul West in his study *The Modern
Novel*, "is obsessed by life's apparently unplanned, mercu-
rial nature: strip us of the poses, roles and responsibilities
we assume, and where are we? What is our identity? Is it
contextual and multiple, or it is as nothing. Verga watches
and reports the hammer-blows; Pirandello, just as determined to be a camera, does X-rays and secretes micro-

phones. His art is encephalographic and almost surreptitious. . . ."

Time and again, Pirandello raised questions that he saw as basic to existence; he did so in a variety of ways. In his plays, through action and confrontation on the stage between actors and actors, actors and directors, actors and the audience; in his novels through forms that ranged all the way from the conventional straight narrative to what today might be called the "essay-novel" and the diary-type fiction. Out of the seven novels he wrote, three have been chosen for discussion in these pages: one from the early period, one from the middle, and the third from his last period, not only because they illustrate clearly the development of his art, but because they are also his most representative and possibly the most lucid artistic statements of Pirandello's vision of the world.

L'esclusa (*The Outcast*, N.Y., 1925) is Pirandello's first novel. It was written between 1893 and 1894, published in serial form in the newspaper *La Tribuna* between June and August 1901, but did not appear in book form until 1908. The magnetism of the book is less its Sicilian setting than the presentation and resolution, so typically Pirandellian as we shall see, of the predicament of the heroine of the story, Marta Pentàgora. We begin by being told that a strange curse seems to hang over the whole Pentàgora family, when Antonio (the father of Rocco, Marta's husband) boldly remarks that the members of his family are all doomed to be betrayed by their wives. Then, through a series of almost ridiculous circumstances, Marta is branded an outcast. Being an outcast is a fundamental condition in Pirandello's world: his characters begin sensing the tragedy of existence precisely when for a variety of reasons they become estranged first from society and ultimately from each other.

The pattern of the conflict that pits the individual against a group, or society at large, is rather carefully presented in Pirandello's first novel. The heroine has been accused of having betrayed her husband with one Gregorio Alvignani, a lawyer and politician. In reality, she is guilty of nothing more than having received some letters from a Sicilian Don

Juan and of having answered them. The letters should really have been taken at their face value, evidence of Gregorio's infatuation on the one hand and of Marta's social impropriety on the other. This rational explanation is unacceptable to Rocco, who must see evil where there was none: after all, the Sicilian code of honor must be respected, and stern punitive action must be taken against the alleged culprit. Marta is forced to leave her home and turns to her family for help. Her father, Francesco Ajala, grieving over the fact that the integrity of his own name has been tarnished by the scandal in which his daughter has become involved, withdraws from his business activities. After his death by apoplexy, the family finds itself financially ruined. Marta's mother and younger sister Maria are in dire need of help, and so Marta finds a position in a local school. The townspeople are not pleased by such a solution; Marta is harrassed, and, this time with the help of Gregorio, finds another teaching position in Palermo. There the story takes a different turn: the two meet as lovers and enjoy momentary respite from the vicious attacks to which they had been subjected. At this point, Rocco's mother (who, as we discover, had experienced the same tragedy as Marta when her jealous husband Antonio had ordered her out of their home) is dying. Marta and Rocco meet at her deathbed and accede to his mother's request to reunite as man and wife. And there is the rub: Marta, accused of the crime of adultery she had never committed is allowed to return home after she has committed the very sin that had caused her to be branded an outcast. Truth has not been allowed to prevail over idle gossips, slanderous accusations, and unjustified suspicion. Ironically enough, the path to reconciliation is open only when an imagined fact has become reality.

Some critics have chosen to see *The Outcast* as one of Pirandello's most thorough attempts to accept the poetics of naturalism. While there is much truth in this view, I would insist that what needs to be stressed is that Pirandello, without rejecting the tradition he had inherited, was hard at work changing it to fit his own special purposes. Thus, the division of the novel in two parts and the fact that the author, as Marziano Guglielminetti perceptively points out, "contrary to the custom of the naturalists, [does not] pursue in [his] exposition of the facts until their chronological development has run its course," are evidences of Pirandello's gradual break from certain established literary conventions. Even the strange balancing technique evident in the structure of the novel (two people die, two babies are born, two different groups of people help Marta in each of the two parts, and so forth), should be seen not as the author's attempt to ape his models, but to give us a sense of the irony of life in a way that seems to anticipate the two stages of his own, and very personal (and in this sense deeply controversial) concept of humor. As the humorist he intended to be, Pirandello devotes the first part to presenting the situation, and sets himself to decompose it in the second. Above and beyond the facts as they are established in the book, we are struck by two points: for all the impressive order society, with its silly traditions, tries to impose upon life, man invariably conducts himself in a most irrational, disorderly fashion. What greater irony could there be in a supposedly naturalist novel than to conclude that lies (or deceptions, or arrangements as variable options open to an individual) by far surpass in value, effectiveness, and acceptability truth itself? Somehow, the novelist subtly suggests, there is something wrong with life if the absence of good will, of compassion and understanding is so widespread. Here Pirandello seems to be in the avant-garde of European novelists in perceiving that the collapse of values that, for better or worse, had governed Western society for several centuries was a central element in the dislocation and disintegration of the human personality. "Never as today," he commented in one of his little-known essays, "was our life more decomposed, aesthetically and ethically. The greater part of our intellectual malaise springs from the centerlessness of our life, which knows no principle of doctrine or of faith, and our thoughts whirl within effective facts. We are waiting, unfortunately in vain, for someone to rise up and announce the *new word*."

In the Sicilian world of taboos, of codes of honor, of

paranoidal jealousy, as well as in the bourgeois world of Rome and other towns, facts do matter, after all. Yet, once we reach the end of *The Outcast* no one wants to think of the immense suffering the fact of Marta's supposed infidelity has caused to so many human beings. No, not even Rocco himself is ready to attach much importance to that fact. "All we have suffered," asks Marta pathetically, "who is going to take that out of our heart?"

Passions for facts, faith in the capacity of science to explain man and hopefully liberate him, are two of the legacies of naturalism. But facts must be placed in their proper context if they are to enable man to reach truth. However, since in Pirandello's scheme of things everything is relative, facts lend themselves, on the one hand, to being manipulated, thus putting the individual on trial and, on the other hand, to being used by the individual to free himself from the constraints of life and create a new existence for himself. The latter possibility is explored in an original manner in Pirandello's third, justly famous novel, *Il fu Mattia Pascal* (*The Late Mattia Pascal*).

The hero of this intriguing novel is Mattia Pascal, a librarian in Miragno, a small provincial town set possibly in Liguria. His life has been unusually unhappy: after his father's death, the family's patrimony has slowly been squandered by his inept mother and his dishonest relatives and Mattia has been forced to accept a minor position which affords him a great deal of freedom but little personal satisfaction. He has been tricked into marrying a woman from his neighborhood, Romilda, who, along with his mother-in-law, now make his life hell on earth. One day Mattia decides to get away for a while from the constant bickering and nagging to which he is subjected every day, and goes to nearby Monte Carlo, taking with him five hundred lire his brother had sent him to take care of the expenses of their mother's funeral. In the city's famous gambling casino, lady fortune is good to Mattia and he wins 82,000 lire, a large sum of money in those days. While he is on the train on his way home, Mattia reads in the town's newspaper a report that his body has been retrieved from a millrace near his property and has been properly identified by his wife. For all intents and purposes Mattia Pascal is dead! Why not take advantage of the situation and try to find a new, happier life for himself? After a period of travel as far as north Germany, Mattia assumes the name of Adriano Meis and decides to settle down somewhere, living the rest of his life in retirement on a fixed income of two hundred lire a month. He first samples life in Milan, but then moves to Rome: "Why Rome and not somewhere else? I see the real reason now. . . . I chose Rome first of all because I liked it more than any other city, and also because it seemed more suited to receive with indifference, among other foreigners, a foreigner like myself." Mattia, in short, decides to live an anonymous life. Much like Marta Pentagora, he becomes an outcast, this time by deliberate choice. He finds a room in the center of Rome with the Paleari family, made up of strange characters indeed: there is the father, Anselmo (a totally inept man), his daughter Adriana, his widowered son-in-law Terenzio Papiano (a swindler and a crook), his brother Scipione (a thief and an epileptic), and a boarder, Silvia Caporale, an ugly, timid music teacher who tries to compensate for her sexual frustration by drinking, and settles down to what he hopes will be a quiet existence. Mattia, at first elated with his newly found freedom, soon enough realizes the distinct limitations of his so-called freedom: he cannot have true friends, for there is too much he has to hide from them; he cannot have a home he can really can call his own; he cannot even have a pet animal, a dog, because that requires a license from the authorities. He looks with increasing disquiet to the possibility of becoming involved in the life of the Paleari, who have shown him respect and affection. "My situation," he notes, "became more and more difficult, the secret embarrassment I had already experienced was now often a piercing remorse, as I saw myself an intruder in their midst, with a false name, altered features, a fictitious and almost nonexistent identity." His relations with the Palearis must therefore remain superficial, particularly when he realizes that his love for Adriana is certain to run into legal difficulties if the two should decide to become man and wife. As this impasse is reached, a substantial amount of money Adriano kept locked in a cupboard in his room mysteriously disappears, as he discovers when he prepares himself to pay the bill for the operation on his eye that presumably made his transformation into Adriano Meis all the more successful. Normally the disappearance, or theft, would be reported to the police authorities. But Adriano's position is hardly normal. On the contrary, it is fraught with all kinds of dangers since in the eyes of the law he has no real identity. He must therefore resort to a lie in order to extricate himself from what is potentially an untenable situation, and reassures everyone that he has found the money. It was, he now claims, in the leather case all the time: he had simply failed to look carefully. Papiano, the culprit (who, probably with his brother's help, stole the money during one of the séances held in the apartment) can breathe more easily. Thanks to his theft, he is now in the position of giving back his father-in-law, Signor Paleari, his late daughter's dowry—a dowry Papiano has recklessly squandered. And it was no great secret that Papiano's attraction to Adriana was motivated by a similar preoccupation. Mattia, on the other hand, realizes he can no longer remain in his *pensione* not only because he must assume that Papiano knows that the money has not been found, and must wonder why Mattia told a lie, but because Mattia cannot go on deceiving Adriana whom he will never be able to marry. Neither his deepest feelings for her, nor his honor (he cannot challenge a man who has publicly insulted him) can have a place in his private or public life, and the only thing left for him to do is to leave and go back to his hometown. But even this cannot be done without disposing of Adriano Meis by faking suicide. He writes his name, Adriano Meis, his address and date on a piece of paper, placing it together with his hat and cane on the parapet of the Margherita bridge over the Tiber, and leaves. Mattia is now dead for the second time: the first, as Mattia Pascal, the second, as Adriano Meis, a "shadow of a life, born from a macabre lie." But the former will have to be resuscitated if Mattia is to have his identity back. He takes the train for Pisa, where he stops off briefly so as to avoid any suspicion between the announcement of the death of Adriano and the reappearance of Mattia, and then stops at Oneglia, where his older brother Roberto makes his home. As is to be expected, Roberto is delighted and surprised to see his brother alive, and promptly informs him of certain important developments that have taken place in Miragno since his presumed death. His wife has remarried, this time to a wealthy man, Pomino, whose temperament is similar to Mattia's, and the couple have been blessed by the birth of a baby girl. His arrival in his hometown is greeted by shock and disbelief: his wife, her new husband, and his cantankerous mother-in-law fear that the happiness they all seem to enjoy will be destroyed. Mattia reassures them on this score: far from wanting his old life back, he declares that he will be happy to spend the rest of his days in retirement, with his old aunt Scolastica, meditating and writing about his past adventures (the subject of the book itself), attempting to understand more clearly the nature of the human predicament. The man who had begun the book by affirming that "one of the few things—perhaps the only one—that I know for certain is that my name is Mattia Pascal," concludes by agreeing with his old friend don Eligio's view that "outside of the law, and without those individual characteristics which, happy or sad as they may be, make ourselves, we cannot exist." Without a legal status, a mere collection of documents, man is doomed to be faceless, his individuality lost in the corridors and offices of inhuman institutions. An "invented" man, a "fictional" human being has no chance to live an authentic life, which requires constant and complex choices no fabricated person can make.

The Late Mattia Pascal's slow pace, the author's propensity to dwell too often and too much on speculative and theoretical philosophical questions, diminish its worth as a powerful statement on life. Indeed, critics have been right in complaining that too much talking about the inner world of Mattia in the long run damages a dramatic rendering of the action. The novel has been called a soliloquy, the story of a man who remembers his trials and tribulations and tries to put the pieces of the puzzle of life together so as to understand it—yet meeting failure at the end. It is no paradox that Mattia ends by admitting that he does not know who he is, and adds laconically "I am the late Mattia Pascal." The problem of the flux of life, our otherness, the sheer impossibility of being free no matter how hard we try, the feeling of seeing life pass us by, limiting and even destroying us as we try to renew ourselves, are the themes— and by no means the only ones—of Pirandello's world. And for no other reasons, *The Late Mattia Pascal*, with all its shortcomings, is an engaging elaboration of Pirandello's manner of looking at the world, an astute development of the theme already stated in *The Outcast*. We have seen how in his first novel, Pirandello presented his heroine Marta as a victim of what in the courts would be called "circumstantial evidence." She owes her downfall to the wholly unjustified inference that she has committed the un-pardonable (in Sicily, at any rate) sin of adultery. On the other hand, Mattia Pascal shows his resourcefulness in turning an erroneous fact to his own advantage. His presumed death allows him to cut his ties with his former life and to everything about it he had come to loathe: his unbearable wife Romilda, his detestable mother-in-law the widow Pescatore, his mediocre job, the narrow-mindedness of the townspeople, and the dishonest manager of what was the Pascals' estate, Signor Malagna.

Once Mattia Pascal has gotten over the initial shock of his new situation, he feels relieved not to be tied to his former obligations and commitments that presumably had prevented him from fulfilling himself. But Mattia, now Adriano Meis, becomes aware of the fact that life has its own special ways of entangling us in the process of being. It is not only problematical, but even impossible to live life standing on the sideline, fooling oneself that by doing so one can remain untouched and unscarred by those experiences that are part of the fabric of life: work, companion-ship, friendships, projects, and the feelings one experiences by living, love, compassion, sorrow, joy. In the last analysis, there cannot be a choice between being and nonbeing, even if all forms of existence prove to be based, to varying degrees, on deceits, lies, accommodations, and compromises. Freed from one set of intolerable personal situations, Mattia-Adriano discovers that to achieve his goal of *vivere, vivere, vivere* ("live, live, live") he cannot avoid human problems. Life demands action and involvement—both of which have their own ways of rewarding and punishing the living individual. Personal freedom turns out to be far more limited than Mattia had anticipated: life makes no provisions for those who manage even for a brief period of time to live what Adriano will call the life of "a loathsome puppet" without any kind of social and legal identity.

One wonders whether, given the special situation alluded to, things could have worked out differently. Giacomo Debenedetti, in an absorbing and rigorous examination of the novel, suggests that "Mattia Pascal should have remained in parentheses, [that is] he should not have reentered society which, fundamentally and structurally, is the same society from which he had exiled himself." In short, Mattia Pascal's changes are too superficial: trimming his beard and undergoing minor surgery to correct his eye make him look different, to be sure. But no amount of cosmetics will change what really must change if he is to become someone else, his inside. And, as Debenedetti perceptively underscores, Pirandello knew only negatively what the new Mattia should be, a "dead" Mattia—hence the significance of the title of the book, *The Late Mattia Pascal*. If life is action, one cannot be suspended in the strange void of nonaction, not for long at any rate, lest one wishes to die.

One of the central qualities of the novel—and, for that matter, of the bulk of Pirandello's work—is the consciousness of living felt through and through by its key characters. As such consciousness becomes more complete, so does the necessity to find a way to fight the oppressive forces society brings to bear on the individual to stifle his freedom. From this vantage point it is clear that "Life," as De Castris observes, in his *Storia di Pirandello*, "is an absurd prison of vain, provisional forms whose result for humanity is oppressive and alienating: society rivets man to a false individuation that warps his wishes and will, thereby breaking up his unity of consciousness into a deceitful multiplicity."

Once the hero of *The Late Mattia Pascal* has disposed of his former self, he starts on a new road that presumably will lead him to his fulfillment as a human being, only to discover that it is impossible to live an unauthentic existence. Since anything is better than nothing, being Mattia is ultimately preferable to being no one.

If Mattia has conveniently exploited his "death," the protagonist of *Uno, nessuno e centomila* exploits life itself, taking the human quest for identity much further than Mattia had ever dared to imagine. That quest is implicit in the structure of the two novels: *The Late Mattia Pascal*, neatly divided into sixteen chapters, two forewords and two addenda, is written as an autobiography that by and large respects the conventions of the genre. *One, None and a Hundred Thousand*, after a traditional beginning moves quickly in the direction of a work composed of a series of connected and frequently dramatized thoughts. Indeed, structurally speaking, the book resembles a work of philosophy and psychology where certain assumptions are constantly tested against the human experience until its logical conclusion is reached. Symmetry is at once striking: the first four books dissolve, layer by layer, the image of the hero's self as it exists in the consciousness of the others; the other four books recount the unusual path Moscarda chooses to construct a more genuine version of what he is. Each book is made up of a varying number of chapters, frequently no longer than a paragraph, each bearing its own title designed to titillate the reader's curiosity. From its first pages the novel quickly moves almost simultaneously in two directions: the telling of a story and the metaphysical considerations and speculations prompted by the events themselves.

Unquestionably the case of Vitangelo Moscarda, the protagonist of *One, None and a Hundred Thousand*, is strikingly different from that of any of the heroes of Pirandello's earlier novels. When he is twenty-eight his drama explodes in full force one day, a day just like any other, when his wife Dida casually remarks that his nose is a bit lopsided. Silly and inconsequential as the observation may be, it unleashes a process of reevaluation of his entire existence. It becomes apparent to him that he is not at all the person he had always assumed himself to be. On the contrary, he is a different Moscarda for each of the people—relatives, friends, business associates, clients—who in one way or another are part of his life. The son of a prominent and highly successful businessman who left him a substantial inheritance invested in the local bank, Vitangelo has never shown much interest in business. In the past he has left the management of his affairs in the hands of his two astute partners, Sebastiano Quantorzo and Stefano Firbo. Yet, while Vitangelo is a moderate, accessible, and considerate gentleman, the fact that, knowingly or not, he condones the exorbitant interest rates his bank charges on the loans extended to its clients makes him appear a despicable usurer, the worthy son of Francesco Antonio Moscarda. The "moment of truth" comes when his wife's innocent remark about his nose makes him realize that there may well be a lot in how he sees himself that does not correspond to what he is as others see him. Unable to reconcile himself to such a dichotomy, Vitangelo opts for a radical alternative: he will destroy with his deeds all those facets of his personality responsible for making him what he is. By doing so, Moscarda believes he will achieve a more accurate definition of what he truly believes himself to be.

The novel thus places one of Pirandello's most dramatic issues squarely on the table: if an individual is not, and cannot be the same for all, since everyone looks at him from a different perspective and in a different context, how can one truly know who he IS? After considering his personal situation, Vitangelo Moscarda comes to the conclusion that everything that took place prior to his wife's revelation must be destroyed. A new beginning is possible only after a *tabula rasa* has been accomplished. The first target in this humorous quest is Moscarda's wife, Dida, for whom he has always been a tranquil, malleable individual. The results of his actions are dramatically effective: Vitangelo's threats, his ill manners, his rude behavior shock Dida to the point of driving her away from their home. Next, Vitangelo begins to change radically the pattern of his relationship with his two business partners, Quantorzo and Firbo, by demanding a thorough account of the bank's activities, intimating that their failure to accede to his request will result in the dissolution of their partnership. (His threat of withdrawing his capital from the bank is eventually carried out, much to the dismay of his family and his partners, and results in the bank's closing down.) Finally—and this decision is viewed most distressingly by all those who thought to know him well —Vitangelo gives notice to an elderly couple, Marco di Dio and his wife Diamante, to vacate a modest apartment where, thanks to his generosity, they have lived for several years without paying any rent. The decision stuns and angers the community, totally unprepared for yet another incredible announcement by Signor Stampa, Moscarda's notary. The couple are to receive in gift a house and the sum of ten thousand lire, thus assuring a comfortable retirement, free of any financial worry.

These actions succeed in destroying the various images people had formed about Vitangelo: that of "Gengè," as his wife affectionately called him; that of "my dear Vitangelo," of his business associates; and that of "the usurer," of his bank's clients. Liberated at last from personalities imposed upon him, Vitangelo may now begin the process of casting an image of what he is closer to what he feels to be true. His peculiar behavior, his bizarre actions have had a serious and negative impact upon all those who knew him. Surely, they begin to say, the man must be insane! Moscarda's reality is not achieved without considerable sacrifice: he has broken the "regularity of his experiences," he has refused to accept history and the traditional theories of cause and effect, thus knowingly cutting the bond that, for good or for evil, ties the individual to his fellowmen.

One day, at the invitation of Anna Rosa, a pretty, twenty-five-year-old friend of Dida, Vitangelo pays her a visit at an appointed place, in the local monastery. She has asked him to meet her, as we find out, to tell him of Dida's scheme to have him committed to an insane asylum with the help of his former business associates and some of the people who have been the recipients of his help. The encounter takes on a sudden, dramatic, and unexpected turn when Anna Rosa drops her purse to the ground and the impact causes a small gun she keeps in her purse to fire and wound her foot. Great consternation follows: the nuns in the monastery are particularly upset by the sight of Vitangelo carrying Anna Rosa in his arms to his house (they do not realize at once that the shooting was accidental) on the very day in which Monsignor Partanna, Bishop of Richieri, is to pay his usual rare, regular visit. Moscarda is undoubtedly attracted to Anna Rosa, and she to him. It is precisely because Anna Rosa is aware of it and tries to avoid the consequences of a possible relationship with him, that when Vitangelo tries to embrace her, she shoots him, this time critically. By agreeing to be declared insane, Moscarda saves Anna Rosa from conviction in a court of law; by donating all his money to the church so that it may build a rest home for the old, the poor, and the sick, and consenting to live among them— outcasts of society—Vitangelo achieves a special freedom he had been denied, and is free at last from the images society had created for, and imposed upon him. He will no longer be what his wife Dida, or his business associates, or his friends, or even his beneficiaries thought he was, but someone else—a pauper content to live the few days left to him (as the wound received is critical) minute by minute, a series of individual, self-contained experiences and feelings unconnected with the past and without links with the future.

No name. No memories today of yesterday's name, or of tomorrow's. I am alive and reach no conclusion. Life does not reach any conclusions. It knows nothing of names. . . . I get out every morning at dawn, because I want to preserve my spirit this way, fresh with dawn, with all things as are barely discovered, when they still preserve the flavor of the night. . . . And the air is new. . . . Only this way can I live now, reborn moment by moment. Preventing my mind from beginning to work inside of me, rebuilding within me the vacuum of empty constructions.

An analysis of Pirandello's opus inevitably compels the attentive reader to make two observations about *Uno, nessuno e centomila*: first, its theme is the logical extension of a view of life articulated in Pirandello's earlier works; second, the formlessness of his last novel is amply justified by the fragmentized existence of its protagonist. The elements of the novel are the same that are found in everything the Sicilian wrote, welding together his short stories, his novels, and his plays: on the one hand, the eagerness of his characters to live a life of possibilities, encounters, surprises, shocks, and discoveries, and, on the other hand, a remarkable sensitivity to the consciousness of living, which takes different shape according to the work itself. In *The Late Mattia Pascal*, for example, it is evidenced by the frequent use of the utterance *"mi vidi"* ("I saw myself"). "My tragedy," explains the protagonist of the short story "La carriola" [The cart], "is this. Whoever lives, as he lives, cannot see himself. . . . If one can see one's own life, this means that he no longer lives it: he bears it, he drags it, he drags it much like something dead. Because every form is death." "When someone lives," affirms Vitangelo Moscarda, "he lives and cannot see himself. To know oneself is to die." "We are born," comments Mattia Pascal, "with a sad privilege: that of feeling ourselves alive. And from this a fine illusion results: We insistently take for eternal reality our inner feeling of life, which varies and changes according to the time, or chance, or circumstances." This feeling of living means a constant effort to define oneself, to project oneself into relationships of various sorts, to be accepted for what we are: yet, few of such understandable goals can be achieved without an open communication with other human beings. And communication is also a major barrier. In the play *Six Characters in Search of an Author* the Father almost shouts to the Director

But don't you see that the whole trouble lies here. In words, words. Each one of us has within him a whole world of things, each man of us his own special world. And how can we ever come to an understanding if I put in the words I utter the sense and value of things as I see them; while you who listen to me must inevitably translate them according to the conception of things each one of you has within himself. We think we understand each other, but we never really do.

As Pirandello matured, and as he perceived more clearly the demands and implications of his vision, he intellectualized his novels at the expense of more traditional renditions of human situations. This tendency prompted E. Allen McCormick to state: "To theorize on one's own life, which is perhaps the outstanding feature of Pirandello's rebels, intentional and unintentional, is to carry a set idea—the point of departure for all the novels—too fully into the life and action of the novels themselves. If there is still value to Henry James' dictum that the novelist should depict and not render, Pirandello failed to appreciate it." Other sympathetic critics have voiced similar objections. Marziano Guglielminetti describes *Uno, nessuno e centomila* a fascinating "collection of soliloquies," while Ulrich Leo calls it "a monologue of notes." Even "when Pirandello wrote 'novels,'" observes Oscar Budel, "they were not novels in the traditional sense: there is no centre, no organized whole, no plot." Precisely. Yet, it is in this very sense that Pirandello was frequently considerably ahead of his times, anticipating not merely the novel of recent years, but some of the techniques, structural and stylistic modes of some of the most celebrated novelists of our century, from Joyce to Sartre, Ionescu, Beckett, and Albee.

In attempting to assess Pirandello's work and his position in the culture of his nation, I have pointed out the singularity of his themes, the originality of their treatment, the persuasive manner in which he gave life to his philosophical preoccupations on the nature of man and his predicament, and the unusual way in which he orchestrated his creative work in a manner that permitted his single pieces to become part of a larger whole. But surely there are many other reasons that commend him to today's readers. For one thing, while born in an era of rationalism, he realized that if science would unquestionably help understand and define human problems, it could never solve them—a lesson our own technologically sophisticated but obtuse society seems unable to accept. He also contributed to making literature, and the novel in particular considered by many readers and critics an idle activity and an inferior genre, a serious instrument of knowledge, capable of illuminating many a truth about man. He resisted the temptations of stylistic embellishments that would no doubt have endeared him to many of his critics and created a dry, nervous, electric style, at times disconnected, replete with questions and exclamations that effectively reflect the temperament of his characters, their anguish, their sufferings, their trepidations and, above all, their doubts. He addressed himself to what is temporary and fragile about existence, the insoluble enigmas, the unanswerable questions of life. Disconsolate as his stance is, there is no despair in his outlook. His short stories, plays, and novels are attempts, limited at times and not always satisfactory, to see man as a whole, man as an end not as a means. Whether one wishes to subscribe to Pirandello's view of the human condition is ultimately irrelevant: what matters, I believe, is that he sought to portray man accidentally or deliberately searching for his essence, realizing his limitations, unafraid to confess his inadequacies, set about to achieve his goal—the retrieval of his own identity—however great and painful the price of his quest would be. Man, as he saw him and depicted long before the official entrance of existentialism on the literary scene, *becomes* through his actions, for which he is responsible. Mattia Pascal and Vitangelo Moscarda are, in this sense, only two of a vast gallery of characters struggling to know themselves in a quest that has its share of humor.

What is ultimately impressive about the work of Pirandello (and not just his novels) is its maker's unflagging determination to confront the irrationality of life itself: his characters not only come to grips with what they are but dare step out in front, on the stage of existence before the jury of the readers, confessing the agony of having to confront conventions that require them to fabricate lies and accept deceits just to go on living. Perhaps this is the example he passed on to those writers who followed him. Those who read him need not be troubled either by his unorthodox attitudes or by his unconventional approach to the problem of existence. Over and beyond his special way of looking at life and of creating characters who address themselves to the ultimate purpose of what they do, Pirandello's work illustrates the necessity of dealing with substantive questions directly and courageously. A "philosophical" writer by instinct and by choice, he sought to express his view of the human condition through the magic of poetry, that is to say through images that convey both the appearances and essence of the problem—thus acknowledging his faith in, and his commitment to art.

9

Federigo Tozzi: The Novel Reborn

> When I think that I am made up of so many bits of experience as I have lived days, I ask myself if I really exist or if it is the objects in front of my eyes that exist. What does it mean, I ask myself, "being alive"?
>
> Tozzi, *Ricordi di un impiegato*

It is frequently said, with some justification, that the fortune or misfortune of a book or a body of literary work changes as regularly, although not as frequently, as the seasons themselves. Perspective and taste are unquestionably two major factors affecting the standing of a writer in any given period, as the changing fortune of, say, Ernest Hemingway, Thomas Mann, William Faulkner, and Herman Hesse forcibly demonstrates. Fortunately time has a way of correcting exaggerated claims originally made about certain books, and different perspectives in turn tend to bring out of obscurity other books which, for one reason or another, deserve to be reconsidered by different sensibilities. Such seems to have been the case of Federigo Tozzi: respected in his lifetime by a mere handful of serious critics, he remained largely ignored by the general public until the end of World War II. Up to that time, the critical response to his work had been tepid and uncertain. Giuseppe A. Borgese, who discovered him, had praised him highly and had linked him with the great tradition of the French and Russian novel. On the opposite side of the critical spectrum, Luigi Russo remarked in his valuable and popular "Baedecker" of modern Italian fiction, *I Narratori: 1850–1957*: "Neither *Tre croci* nor *Il podere* seem to us to be masterpieces; and we cannot speak of them as minor masterpieces since to have such qualifications art must have a unity and a cohesion of motives lacking in Tozzi ['s books]."

In recent years, the tide seems to have been reversed, thanks largely to the concerted efforts of several critics who have set out to reappraise the worth of much of contemporary Italian fiction. As a result, Tozzi has been reread carefully and rediscovered, as it were. A closer examination of his literary production has considerably enhanced his position in the literary firmament of Italian letters to the point that one of his most recent admirers, Alberto Moravia, has called him "the fourth [great] Italian novelist, together with Manzoni, Verga, and Svevo." Although most of Tozzi's work was published between 1917 and 1921, the first three volumes of his *opera omnia* edited by his son Glauco appeared only in 1961–63, together with a valuable apparatus that clarifies many thorny questions of chronology, spelling, and revisions, thus paving the way for a fairer evaluation of his work. Outside of Italy, too, Tozzi's reputation has slowly been growing: some of his short stories have appeared in English, and he has been hailed, together with Verga and Svevo, as "one of the masters of Italian narrative since the Unification of Italy." His memorable novella *Ricordi di un impiegato* recently appeared in English (*Journal of a Clerk*, N.Y., 1964) and still another of his major novels, *Con gli occhi chiusi* [Blindfolded], is being translated and will soon be brought out by a major university press.

The seriousness of Tozzi's fiction, the depth of his insights, his sober style through which he so brilliantly translates onto the written page the schizophrenic or paranoiac temperament of his characters, more than amply compensate for what some may call a limited vision. Seldom before him has the Tuscan countryside been painted in such splendid and yet foreboding ways, and even more rarely have Italian novelists succeeded in recapturing the violence, the squalor, and the loneliness of existence in a provincial town as successfully as he. The reader ready not to be dismayed by the singularly awkward and ungrammatical style of Tozzi, with its special Sienese words and expressions carefully reproduced in their spelling, will find his fiction rewarding for the completeness in which his statements on life are articulated.

Comparisons and parallels with other writers are frequently, if not irrelevant, invidious. Yet, there is much that Tozzi has in common with such contemporaries as Verga, Svevo, and Pirandello, whose work he admired and by whom he was respected. With Verga, Tozzi shares a realistic, unpretentious style as well as a brutally honest manner of looking at life; with Svevo, he shares not only a defiance of *il bello scrivere*, but a commitment to explore the psyche of his characters, giving their actions a psychological justification; and, finally, with Pirandello he shares considerable skepticism vis-à-vis human nature: "I do not believe any other writer feels as much as Pirandello that evil and meanness [are] natural conditions that cannot be abolished," he wrote about the Sicilian master. A careful reading of Tozzi's work bears out how much such a comment is pertinent to his own vision of the world.

Similarly, Tozzi's life supplies us with stunning evidence of the pain and loneliness so dramatically mirrored in his fiction. His father, Domenico, came from peasant stock and was a prosperous farmer as well as the owner of a renowned restaurant called "Trattoria del Sasso." His mother, Annunziata, was a melancholy woman who had experienced more than her share of grief, having lost eight children shortly after their birth before having Federigo in 1883. She herself was to die of an epileptic attack in 1895 with disastrous results for her only surviving child. The beatings regularly administrated by his father and the moody character of his mother had anything but a positive effect upon young Federigo, himself frequently ill. That he was quite unhappy with his home life is obvious by the mediocrity of his school work and his lack of interest in his father's business. According to one of his few intimate freinds, Domenico

Giulotti, Federigo "could neither rinse glasses nor prepare the bill for the customers." The clientèle of his father's restaurant considered him unbalanced, a person with criminal tendencies who, "in the best case, would have ended up in a criminal asylum." Young Federigo managed to complete his elementary schooling and was subsequently enrolled in a local religious school from which he was expelled a few years later because of his unruly behavior. Thanks to his mother's efforts, he was enrolled in a Fine Arts institute, from which he was expelled for his poor academic performance. Again with his mother's help, he was accepted at a technical institute in Arezzo and managed to win his diploma. For a while, after having matriculated in a private school, he studied on his own, only to fail in Italian and drawing when he took his exams in Florence. His mother's death had left him to the care of a father who was temperamentally and culturally incapable of coping with Federigo's anormal character and artistic aspirations. Between 1899 and 1903, Tozzi had his first love affair with a young peasant girl, Isola: some of the strange episodes of that affair were to be fictionalized in one of his most singular novels, *Con gli occhi chiusi*. His political ideas were evolving and he became a Socialist, a move that predictably strained even further his relationship with his father. Surprisingly enough, when Federigo decided to try his luck in Rome, his father helped him financially, never anticipating that as a result of such a trip his son would break with socialism, a party he opposed.

Shortly before the end of his affair with Isola, Federigo had met Emma Palagi, and the two became engaged. The letters they exchanged during their long courtship appeared posthumously, in 1925, in a volume titled *Novale*. In Rome, his job hunting proved to be unproductive and frustrating. Several months later he was back in Siena and to his constant clashes with his father. In 1907, wishing to marry Emma, Tozzi entered a national competitive examination for a civil service job with the post office. He failed that examination, but passed another exam for a post with the state railroads. On March 5, 1908, he left for Pontedera, a small town on the western seaboard of Tuscany where he had been assigned; two months later, he was transferred to Florence. His experience was to inspire his first novella, *Ricordi di un impiegato*, published in an edited version in 1920 by his literary mentor Giuseppe Borgese. Barely three weeks after his transfer to Florence, he was called to the bedside of his dying father. For some years, Federigo considered the possibility of making his home in his native city. But even that modest dream was quickly shattered by the harassment of people who claimed to be his illiterate father's creditors. In 1914 he sold the restaurant and one of his two farms, rented the other, and together with his wife and small son, Glauco, left for Rome, where he hoped to find a job as a newspaperman. The following year, at the outbreak of World War I, he volunteered for service in the press office of the Red Cross to begin yet another unhappy period of his life. By that time he had already published two slim collections of poetry, *Zampogna verde* [Green bagpipe] (1911) and the poem *La città della Vergine* [The city of the Virgin] (1913), both written under the influence of d'Annunzio. Yet, he was known only to a small group of intellectual friends. During his brief visits to Siena, Tozzi managed to complete several manuscripts. Although few of his pieces were accepted, he did not give up. In 1917, thanks to the intervention of Giuseppe Borgese, the influential literary critic of the Milanese daily *Il corriere della sera*, Tozzi's book *Bestie* [Animals] was accepted by the prestigious publishing house of Treves & Co. Two years later, after a delay caused by some uncomplimentary remarks Tozzi had made about d'Annunzio (Treves's best-selling author), his first full-length novel, *Con gli occhi chiusi*, written in the latter part of 1913, appeared in print. Nineteen eighteen proved to be an exceedingly productive year for Tozzi: he wrote about half of *Il podere* (July 3–24) and finished *Tre croci* (*Three Crosses*, N.Y. 1921) (October 25–November 9). Before the end of 1919, he had also completed *Gli egoisti* [The egotists] and had rewritten his earlier novella, *Ricordi di un impiegato*, originally written in 1910.

Even though he both loved and hated his native city, he

returned there at regular intervals. Much like Leopardi's Recanati, Tozzi drew considerable inspiration from Siena, its lovely surroundings, and its inhabitants. In the winter of 1920 he fell ill with pneumonia. He was brought back to his tiny apartment in Rome, and there he died on March 21. His sudden death robbed him of the satisfaction of seeing his two major novels in print. *Tre croci* was brought out a few weeks after he had passed away, followed by *Il podere* in 1921 and two years later by *Gli egoisti*. A volume of his critical essays, with the title *Realtà di ieri e di oggi*, appeared in 1928.

Tozzi's sudden death was sorrowfully noted by fellow writers and a few critics who had understood that his fiction had marked the entrance in the world of letters of an important artist. It is difficult to understand why, aside from the occasional commemorative pieces (in which Italians excel) and the work of a handful of critics, Tozzi should be so quickly brushed aside. Was it the historical moment? Yes, if one remembers that the group of the Roman magazine *La Ronda* had been devoting its vitality to a stylistic return to the classicism of Leopardi and Manzoni. For them Tozzi's rough, lean style could hardly stir much enthusiasm and admiration. Was Tozzi's own neurotic character another factor in the silence that enveloped the Sienese novelist after he died? At least one of his admirers, Giose Rimanelli, takes this position in his eclectic volume *Il mestiere del furbo*. Unquestionably, Tozzi could not be a writer with a large following: he lacked the dash and rhetoric of d'Annunzio, the ability of Pirandello to orchestrate his literary production around the fascinating, philosophical problem of reality and appearances, the bombastic egocentricity of Giovanni Papini, one of the most polemical, loud and intellectually vulgar writers of the 1910s and 1920s. Masters can afford to wait, however, for they speak to their own but even more to future generations. Their case, as it were, may rest—but it may not be written off.

The world of Federigo Tozzi is already and unmistakably sketched out in many of the short stories he began writing as early as 1908, a full decade before the completion of the bulk of his novels. Beyond any question, his is a sensual, highly volatile, proud, and, above everything else, violent world, where men and women fall victims of their passionate desires, have their share of erotic or tragic adventures, and frequently long, or so it seems, to fulfill their death wish. In "Assunta" (1908), for example, we confront a woman who has many of the typical traits of Tozzi's heroines: she is beautiful, amoral, sensual, totally incapable to stop dreaming of being physically possessed by as many men as possible. Understandably enough, Marco is extremely jealous of his bride-to-be, all the more since he suspects, with ample justification, that she is carrying on with Domenico, the son of a moderately well-to-do family of farmers. His suspicions proved to be well-founded: when Assunta does not deny that she and Domenico have been together, he strikes her. When Domenico suddenly arrives on the scene and attempts to free Assunta from Marco's grip as he is trying to strangle her, Marco stabs him in the heart and kills him.

Violence of another sort prevails in yet another story, "Il ciuchino" [The little donkey] (1908), the tale of a newborn donkey that is forced to die by its mother, who refuses to nurse it. Set for the most part in a humble stable, it is a striking tale bound to recall a similar and well-known story by Giovanni Verga, "Storia dell'asino di San Giuseppe." But while Verga's tale is one of exploitation (the donkey passes from one owner to the next, always decreasing in value as its health deteriorates, always doomed to harder and more miserable work until, one day, it drops dead on the road, at which point his carcass is sold for the price of its hide) Tozzi's is one of alienation, of total rejection by the very creature that has given birth to the protagonist of the *racconto*. The rejection is unexplained, mysterious, but just the same tragic, a source of misery and of death. The estrangement of Roberto Falchi, the hero of another story, "Musicomane" [Musicmaniac] (1908), is certainly more understandable, if only because his mental retardation is caused by an acute case of meningitis. After his illness,

Falchi abandons his studies that will prepare him for a professional career, and spends his time meandering all over the town, prey of an illness that knows no cure, object now of pity, now of jest on the part of the passersby.

The texture of Tozzi's tales is a strange mixture of the pathetic and the sarcastic, the haunting and the hallucinatory; the author's attitude shifts nervously from hostility to a Christian resignation and warm compassion for the victims of life. The tension created in his tales is electric, much like that of two wires always exposed to and eventually touching each other, thus setting off the spark that sets off the sound and fury of the action.

Death is also the culmination of another short story, "Ozio" [Idleness] (1910), revolving around the visit paid to a farm by two city dwellers, Gastone and his wife, Giovacchina, to Enrico, his wife Gemma, and her stepmother. After a rather gluttonous repast, they all decide to take a nap on the grass, under the shade of a large chestnut tree. The chirping of a bird awakens their interest, and they begin a short chase to capture the little thing. Having caught it at last, they first wonder whether they should release it from its brief captivity; then Gastone takes its little head between his index finger and his thumb and squashes it.

Adulteresses, idiots, paralytics, peasants doomed to a wretched existence, brothers and sisters alienated from one another to the point of driving each other relentlessly to the grave, menial clerks, gross, insensitive farmers—such are the characters that live in the pages of Tozzi's short stories. The prevailing mood is somber, frequently morbid, and bordering on a kind of despair a human being experiences when, for some mysterious reason, he has lost the will to live. "I have a desire to cry [so strong] that it upsets me. I feel my heart so sad and so tired, that I do not know how I am capable of living," confesses the protagonist of another of Tozzi's early short stories, "Un ragazzo" [A Boy] (1914?). Once again, his tale of sad events is narrated both simply and detachedly. He feels unwanted and hated by his father, whose affection he desperately needs now that his mother has passed away.

His father, instead, maltreats him, demeans and beats him constantly, making him pay physically for his shortcomings and for what he sees as unbearable ignorance and arrogance. He is finally disowned by his father, who names his servant Giulia who has become his mistress, the heiress of his property.

Such and other short stories by Tozzi reveal some of his early preoccupations and prepare us for his novels. Indeed, it comes as no surprise to us to find that the hero of *Ricordi di un impiegato* (*Journal of a Clerk*) shares much of the same temperament of his predecessors. But the links go even further: Leopoldo Gradi, such is the name of the protagonist of Tozzi's novella, lives out a life not of action but of feelings: his relationship with his father, marked by misunderstandings, his paranoiac sense of being threatened by the town where he has moved, his loneliness, and his general fear of life. Written in the form of a diary irregularly kept between one January 3 and one April 22, the work has hardly a plot. The simple story it tells, however, has a Kafkaesque quality about it. Leopoldo is practically forced by his father to accept a post with the state railroad at Pontedera. Accepting the job means to leave his family and his fiancée Attilia, who in the diary appears less a real person than a transparent symbol of the tranquility for which Leopoldo yearns. Once in Pontedera, Leopoldo finds it difficult to adjust himself to the new milieu. One day, quite unexpectedly, he receives a letter informing him that Attilia is serious ill. His request for a short leave is approved, and he sets off for Florence in time to see his newly born sister while finding his fiancée Attilia dead. "The desolation of the scene," writes F. N. Cimmino, "has a reflection of the same intonation on the face of his mother, who has recently given birth to a baby girl; life and death run after each other; they remain naturally different, but have the same flavor." Now that life has taken such a different turn, Leopoldo begins wishing that he would not have to go back to Pontedera. With his father's approval, his wish is fulfilled. Leopoldo's tormented diary ends with this laconic note: "I am staying in Florence."

Much like the bulk of Tozzi's literary production, the novella is to some extent autobiographical less because of the obvious parallels with the private events of its author, than for the sense of estrangement and isolation its protagonist experiences.

> Every time a man I do not know comes near me I'm afraid of him, sometimes even when he's a friend. It is not exactly the man I'm afraid of, but rather of what may happen to me, deep inside me, when he starts to speak. For this reason there are certain people I have always kept away from. I remember I used to walk on a road just outside Florence; I had to pass by a green garden gate. Whenever I saw the gardener standing there by the open gate, I either turned back or passed by the opposite side of the road. Anything to avoid having to come into contact with him.
>
> There are people who would be astonished to learn what ineffaceable marks they have left on me. When I think that I am made up of as many bits of experience as I have lived days, I ask myself if I really exist or if it is the objects in front of my eyes that exist. What does it mean, I ask myself, "being alive"?
>
> Why can't I ever forget the years I have lived—years scattered here and there like the moss that clings to stones?

It should be noted that the figure of the clerk is a popular one with naturalism. To limit ourselves to the Italian scene, the most obviously similar character is to be found in Svevo's novels *Una vita* (1892; *A Life*, N.Y., 1963) and *Senilità* (1898; *As a Man Grows Older*, N.Y., 1932). But the comparison between Leopoldo and his counterparts Alfonso Nitti and Emilio Brentani cannot be pressed too far: Svevo's characters entertain dreams that prove to be unrealizable because of their ineptness, their lack of initiative, their incapacity to exploit those opportunities that could easily change the course of their lives. Svevo's irony is possible precisely because of such a contrast, as well as a persistent inability to read life realistically, as it were. On the other hand, Leopoldo only senses a secret hostility toward him, which becomes a barrier that is all but unsurmountable. There cannot be any rapport between himself and the people whom he meets but who immediately repel him. Incapable of relating to anyone, Leopoldo withdraws to his little "hole," resigned to be inescapably unhappy. He is, of course, trapped in a situation which is not of his own making and over which, as a mere clerk, he has no control: he has an insignificant job in an alien environment, victim of the manipulations first of his father, then of his supervisor. "The remedy [for his infected personality, his wrong behavior]," observes Debenedetti, "consists precisely in avoiding finding a remedy: Leopoldo's human definition is all here." It is here that Tozzi offers us more than a glimpse of the changing technique of the novel. Plot is subjugated to character study, dialogue gives way to monologues, reality is seen with the distorted lenses of a neurotic or a psychological misfit. Man no longer has the upper hand on life, by which he is emotionally and psychologically subdued. The crudest scenes, the most trivial incidents, are magically transformed into extremely effective tools to illuminate man's character. At one point, Leopoldo counts his shorts, his underwear, and his socks as though he were actually attempting to take stock of what he is. Tozzi's characters think very little or too highly of themselves, and much of their time is actually spent in tormenting themselves, gnawing, and even physically destroying each other. "So I have alienated myself from this kind of reality," confesses Leopoldo. "Why, why? Why have I shut my soul like this? Even when I was a boy I liked to be alone; I used to like standing at a half-open door watching the people in a room talking. I regret what I do and yet I keep on doing the same thing. I am hungry, but I don't eat; yet I like this sense of kindly reality that always returns as though it were in love with me."

In the novels, as in many of his short stories, Tozzi's heroes are by necessity always engrossed in some sort of money-making activity in which they fail miserably. We see them, small merchants or farmers, living comfortably or even beyond their means, intent on making sure that their bellies are full even if they cannot satisfy their emotional needs. Losers in what they do and failures in what they are is their common denominator. Because they are bent on a senseless self-destruction, they deny themselves the air they need, the bread they must eat to survive, the love and compassion for which they frequently yearn. Fate inexorably denies them both peace of mind and compassion for human suffering. Seldom are Tozzi's characters granted a respite from the anguish of living or the chance to communicate to others their inner torment. There is no way to work out problems, and even when a dialogue begins it soon degenerates into an angry confrontation.

If *Ricordi di un impiegato* succeeds in setting up the general climate of mistrust and dishonesty that prevails in much of Tozzi's fiction, *Con gli occhi chiusi* provides the key to the fundamental theme of his novels. The story the book tells is definitely drawn from its author's life. The locales, Siena and Florence, were places where he had spent much of his youth; the characters are modeled upon people he had known first-hand. Pietro, the main character, is Tozzi himself; Ghísola (after whom the novel was originally entitled) is Isola, the author's first love; Domenico and Anna (Pietro's parents) bear much more than a casual resemblance to Domenico and Annunziata, right down to their occupation. But there is something far more central to our understanding of Tozzi's novels that finds its proper place in *Con gli occhi chiusi*, and it has to do with the complicated, tortuous relationship between Pietro and his father with the element that sets it on its course. Everything else in the book is subordinated to such a relationship and overshadowed by it.

When the book opens, the protagonist is a mere thirteen-year-old boy; his mother, whose previous seven children have died at various times shortly after birth is an epileptic; his father is the proprietor of a modest but highly renowned restaurant in Siena, the "Pesce Azzurro." Anna's health, already precarious, deteriorates after an accident at the restaurant (when her husband narrowly escapes being stabbed to death by a drunk customer), and on the advice of her doctor, she goes to live in their nearby farm, together with Rebecca (Pietro's wet nurse and Domenico's mistress), her parents Giacco and Masa, and, a few years later, their niece Ghísola.

For a number of reasons, some of them having to do with his health, Pietro's studies do not proceed well at the local seminary, and eventually he is asked by the principal to leave the school. His friendship with Ghísola is at least a modest consolation for his loneliness and general unhappiness: his mother, feeling guilty for her illness, barely manages to talk with him; Domenico, contemptuous toward education, disappointed and even angered by his son's poor scholastic record, is hardly a father to him. With his mother's permission, Pietro enrolls in a technical school of fine arts. Just when his mother decides to take him to the parish priest to discuss their plan, she dies quite suddenly and Pietro's situation worsens considerably. Domenico now finds himself entirely responsible for his son's upbringing and his education. The two have preciously little in common: Pietro lacks his father's aggressiveness, his ambition, his toughness of manners and living, and is therefore ill-suited for the sort of job his father has in mind for him as the manager of the family's inn. What at first appeared as a simple difference of temperament soon explodes into an open antagonism and even hostility when Domenico realizes that his son will have no part of his plans and will not accept the task of managing the inn. Even three years later, when Pietro has finally achieved his degree, Domenico finds him "useless to [his] interests, like any other idiot!" His spirit undampened, Pietro continues studying on his own for a year, having already been accepted by a technical school in Florence. This time, however, the event marks "the total disappearance of any tie between the father and his son. More and more, they treated one another like two strangers forced to live together." Unable to bear the sense of guilt and shame for still being considerably behind in his studies, and not wishing to live near a person who rejects him, Pietro takes a room in Florence. His situation, however, is hardly one conducive to a tranquil existence, and he begins brooding over his past, full of sorrow and neglect, his lonely present, and his uncertain future. Those who live around him cannot change his predicament: "He realized that he had tried, in vain, to become closer to his friends; his indifference toward some changed into hostility and enmities; he felt an aversion toward everyone, especially those who were rich and who esteemed him very little because he was a Socialist. Most people thought he was crazy; but almost everyone was fond of him."

After some years spent away from the farm at Poggio de' Meli, Ghísola returns and has an affair first with one of Pietro's boyhood friends, Borio, then with his overseer, and with other men. In order to avoid a scandal, Ghísola is persuaded to leave town and becomes the mistress of Alberto, a small merchant who is himself separated from his wife. Pietro, of course, cannot reconcile himself to the idea that the girl he thinks he loves has left him. After taking his exams, he goes to the farmhouse where Ghísola is kept by her lover. Alberto, realizing that he is much older than his mistress and that his precarious financial situation has deteriorated substantially (he files for bankruptcy before too long), suggests that Ghísola exploit Pietro's naïveté and make him believe that he is the father of the child she is bearing. When Pietro refuses to make love to her, she becomes terrified by the prospect of having to account for a child without a father and runs away to Florence. An anonymous letter informs Pietro of Ghísola's whereabouts. And it is in a house for expectant mothers and prostitutes that he finally finds her. At last Pietro understands the reality of the situation: the shock of seeing Ghísola pregnant is too much for him. He faints at her feet: he now knows that he no longer loves her.

As is frequently the case with Tozzi, the story of *Con gli occhi chiusi* is simple and linear. Yet, its simplicity does not make it an easy book; on the contrary, it serves as an effective contrast with the psychological complexity of the characters of the novel. The tensions at work begin in a low key and gain momentum as the morbid, murky story develops in its provincial setting. There are tensions everywhere: between Domenico and his customers and his employees, between father and son, between Pietro and his playmates and Ghísola herself. Each relationship carries within the possibility of psychological confrontations. The central point of the book and what turns out to be the leitmotif of Tozzi's novels, is to be found in the very title of the book—*Con gli occhi chiusi* [Blindfolded], a perfectly convincing emblem of his world view. Borgese, reviewing the novel, spoke of its being "too autocritical," alluding "frankly to a method of austere introspection, a relentless examination of conscience, in which the author implicates the other characters and landscapes with himself." Actually, as Debenedetti has brilliantly shown, Tozzi's novels are the extensions and dramatizations in a psychological key of a single theme, the traumatic conflict between a neurotic human being and his intolerant, unsympathetic, and insensitive father.

It is in this context that we begin to realize how Tozzi, himself an admirer and a perceptive reader of Giovanni Verga, offers a modern treatment of the ancient question of *la roba*, property. While in Verga's masterpieces *I Malavoglia* and *Mastro-don Gesualdo* the drive to improve one's own economic lot inevitably leads to their ultimate defeat all those ready to forsake the "religion of the home" and the "ideal of the oyster" (and its tenacious attachment to its shell), in Tozzi's novels property is shown as no longer acceptable as a valid yardstick of man's real worth. Quite the opposite: material possessions, far from being an asset, are actually a detriment for they obfuscate the real issue of how man can be socially and morally defined. As such, property must be rejected, refused, and denied if one is to find one's own identity in a confused and confusing world. Thus, years before the school of the Absurd, Tozzi was writing novels whose climate and themes are distinguished by a willful and pronounced lack of commitment to a life of property, by an estrangement from middle-class values. Time and again, Pietro is depicted as being "absent," "distracted," disinterested, as it were, from accepted standards of social worth, an attitude that reflects a peculiarly contemporary uneasiness in living in a world that has mysteriously ceased to have much attraction to man. Like Pietro, most of Tozzi's characters behave strangely or erratically, leading an existence that, for all its realism, is often incomprehensibly cut off from the ordinary ways of men. Indeed, it is even possible for some readers to sympathize (although the term is not appropriate from a moral position) with Pietro's father, who does not hesitate to beat his son, scold him, and insult him, according to the circumstances, hoping that he might succeed in bringing him back to the world of money, sex, and violence in which he thrives with considerable success.

The figure of the father, with his propensity to castrate his son most likely to usurp his power, is very central in Tozzi's major novels, particularly *Con gli occhi chiusi*. But even when he is not there physically, he is nevertheless ever-present like a curse one cannot forget, a part of the past one cannot eradicate from his memory—a symbol of what must ultimately be destroyed, at whatever cost, if one is to become liberated from the nightmares of one's youth.

The protagonist of *Il podere* [The farm], Remigio Selmi, is coming home, unexpectedly and urgently summoned to the bedside of his moribund father Giacomo. In Tozzi's fiction, the theme of the return to the homestead assumes a special meaning, for it is a return to a home that has always lacked its traditional security and its association with the warmth of love and happiness. One returns home, an empty, desolate, forbidding shell, not to live but to die. And Remigio will die, in the very last paragraphs of the book, at the hand of a discontented farmhand, Berto, in what is yet another of a numerous list of incomprehensible, absurd facts that take place in the tale.

The "odor" of death and of decay, already present in the opening scene of the book, permeates the entire work. Summoned home from his post at the Campiglia railroad station (we are never told specifically what his functions there are), Remigio sneaks into his father's bedroom, and is at once scolded by two of the farmhands for the manner in which he has chosen to arrive. Death and hostility, humiliation and incomprehension will remain, throughout the story, recurrent motifs and attitudes. Like Pietro's father (in *Con gli occhi chiusi*), Giacomo, too, is a well-to-do farmer who has succeeded not only in tripling the estate he inherited upon his father's death, but in commanding the respect of those who work for him. After the death of his first wife (Remigio's mother), Giacomo took a country hick, Giulia, as his mistress. Soon afterward, wishing to stop once and for all local gossiping, he married Luigia. For all practical purposes, their marriage ends when Luigia's place in the matrimonial bed is usurped by Giulia. Giacomo is now at the end of his life: a gangreneous infection in his foot is rapidly spreading throughout his blood, and he is beyond help. Doctor Umberto Bianchini, a local surgeon, is asked to intervene. He, too, however, like the rest of the characters in the story, turns out to be just another exploiter of human misery, who does not hesitate to look out for his interests by prescribing medicines he knows to be useless and making frequent calls on his patient only to pad his already high bill for services rendered.

Immediately after Giacomo's death, the schemes to cheat Remigio begin. People furiously demand that their accounts be settled, their bills rendered, their back salaries paid, even though there is no possible way to check the legitimacy or veracity of their claims. Giulia herself, banned from the farm, seeks revenge with the help of Boschini, a lawyer of dubious reputation. With the assistance of two false witnesses who wish to engage in a personal vendetta against Giacomo's son only because of their personal grudge against the dead man, Giulia demands payment of a large sum of money, eight thousand liras, she claims represents a loan extended to her lover several months before his death plus six years of back pay. The scheme is obviously fraudulent, but without documents or witnesses to disprove the claim, Remigio is forced into an untenable legal situation. Luigia, a vulgar and insensitive woman, looks upon him with increasing suspicion, despite the fact that there is absolutely nothing in what Remigio does or says to justify even remotely the dishonesty of which she accuses him. Clearly Remigio is inept, he is incompetent in the devious ways of the business world. His naïveté makes him an easy prey of all those who try to persuade him that they are on his side, eager to help him get out of his predicament, while in effect conspiring to destroy him. He never succeeds in understanding the incomprehensible, nasty, and hostile world into which he has been thrust. He never succeeds in establishing a meaningful rapport either with the people who work for him and who resent him, or his relatives who mistrust him, or even his own lawyer, Neretti, charged with the responsibility of protecting his rights and safeguarding his interests. Remigio seems to be perennially, literally and metaphorically, on trial, always at a loss to provide the documents and witnesses any court of law requires or the confidence in his integrity without which no human bond can be established. Remigio is as incapable of penetrating the secret that has contributed to the success of his father as he is of grasping the puzzling laws inexorably turned against him. He is ridiculed by his own attorney, antagonized by his farmhands, suspected by those who should have a measure of faith in his decency. His predicament is summed up in an observation the author makes shortly before most of his disasters fall upon him: "His whole life seemed shut in a sack, from which there was no way to pull his head out."

As the story unfolds and the complexities unravel one after the other, we see that an extra element, this time totally independent from human machination, is unleashed with all its furies against Remigio. The weather has now joined those men and women who are conspiring to deny Remigio a bare moment of well-being, at least a glimpse of contentment and serenity. Whether by thievery, or spite, or natural causes, all prospects of a good harvest are cancelled. First a small crop of cherries suddenly vanish from the tree that stands right in front of Remigio's bedroom window; then a violent rainstorm damages the haystacks and rots half of the crop; then the already critical situation is worsened when a fire, apparently mysteriously started by an unknown person (we discover that the culprit is another of Remigio's enemies, Chiocciolino), burns a good part of the harvest of wheat. A small calf, purchased at the monthly fair in Siena at the insistence of Picciòlo, almost dies, while a cow miscarries, thus extending the initial preoccupation with death. Without the affection of whatever family Remigio has left, constantly harassed in the courts by his father's mistress and by one of her false witnesses who tries to extort two hundred liras for two pigs he claims Giacomo never paid for, the protagonist slowly realizes that he has no one in whom to confide. Riddled by debts and by the promissory notes he is forced to sign in order to have the necessary cash to meet his increasingly longer list of obligations, Remigio loses heart. His farm, poorly cared for by the farmhands, parched by the sun, falls into neglect and becomes an intolerable burden.

All throughout the unfolding of the story, the reader is bound to ask whether there is indeed a reason for the inequities and injustices victimizing Remigio. The answer, or at least *an* answer, is provided by something that Dr. Bianchini tells Giulia, who is asking him for help. The doctor speaks in harsh terms about Remigio: "For me," he says, "a son who goes away from his home, whatever his reasons may be, must be punished. His duty was to remain in the family and obey his father, because he would have been better off that way. He had no right to go against his father's will." The statement has Verghian overtones: leaving one's home is equivalent to betraying the ideals of the family, the legacy of values of our forefathers. By departing, man breaks the continuity and the order of the *casa*, becoming uprooted and eventually estranged not merely from the world about him, but from his very self. "I believe," affirms Berto at one point, "that [all] these things never happen without God's wishes." A kind of a curse seems to hang over Remigio's life, made wretched by circumstances he cannot control and by a sin he must expiate by his sufferings and his eventual death, anticipated by a stark passage notable for his gloom and sadness:

This time, however, he could not hope in anything; and he abandoned himself to his own feelings. Why had he not fled that night when his farm was burning? Why had he returned to Siena, if his father wanted to die without letting him know it? Why had he become the owner of the Casuccia [estate] almost by subterfuge? He feared something unknown, more consistent than his own soul. But, although he had not thought of God for many years, he could not believe that God wanted to annihilate him in that way. What had he done wrong? Why could not his will exist? . . . He thought also of all the people he knew who had died without his caring. He too could now die, and no one would mourn him.

It is Remigio's fate to exist in a world beyond his rational, or emotional comprehension, in an incoherent, tragic world of discord, anger, and hatred. It is hatred, indeed, that eventually causes the hero's downfall, a hatred that is traceable to nothing more than envy, resentment, and arrogance. It is no wonder then why, to the very end of his drama, Remigio's important question, "Why does he [Berto, his future murderer] hate me?" should go unanswered: there is no rational explanation to the chain of misfortunes that fall upon him. The mystery of fate defies penetration, just as there is no escape from such a sordid, hopeless world. Much like the work of Beckett, the tension of Remigio's drama lies precisely in his feeling of impotence, of powerlessness in finding a reason for his futile existence. Evil is heaped upon evil, wrong upon wrong, and there is no end to it: for there is evil not only among the creditors, the notaries, the lawyers, the farmhands who take an active role in the systematic destruction of Remigio, but there is evil in his own intense desire to destroy the inheritance left to him by his father: the land, the house, the animals—the things, *la roba* that rather than making his life easier make it monstrously unbearable. Once again, Tozzi's private trauma finds its expression in the novel: the denial of those values based upon a system of possessions is effectively turned into a denial of what they represent, a paternal power that destroys rather than builds the ego of the son. It matters little whether the relentless destruction that erodes Remigio's power is self-imposed or brought on by inexplicable forces.

The defeat to which he seems doomed from the very beginning is traceable to his inability to surrender what he has not really earned. And it is precisely in such a struggle, which will climax with Remigio's death, that we see mirrored the sociopolitical battle that was to intensify after the end of World War I. The farmhands emerge as a force opposing and eventually fighting a bourgeois system of values they consider unjust and abhorrent. As Tozzi presents his story, we know that the theme will be developed in a vertical manner. The conflict will not follow a linear development: it will only be intensified, worsening the already poisonous air everyone breathes. Remigio must go down to defeat without uttering a single word: he never understood, much less developed a capacity to rebel against his fate, and it is therefore natural that he should be unable to perceive the reason for the chain of disasters that eventually wreck his life. Like Remigio, most of Tozzi's characters in the novel are failures because, in the words of Ferruccio Ulivi, they have displayed an "inability to catch by surprise, and bend adroitly and cunningly" the land itself, the soil that can yield its harvest only when it is mastered by man. "When nature, the soil, is confronted by someone who is timid or inexperienced, it reacts like human society ruining even its best harvest."

Il podere tells the tale of the wretched existence of a young man whose ineptness causes his downfall, but whose sudden death can be ascribed only to the inexorable, inexplicable laws of fate. *Tre croci* (*Three Crosses*, N.Y., 1921), certainly the most objective novel Tozzi wrote, is linked to the earlier narratives through the theme of failure. This time, however, the heroes—all failures—are three and the story of their ruin begins as all of them rapidly approach their end. The violent, primitive world of the farm, the wrath and contempt of the farmhands, the ignoble machinations of lawyers, notaries, and false witnesses, give way to a more bourgeois, but equally sordid world of the Gambi brothers. This time the tables are turned: it is no longer a secret conspiracy that drives the three brothers to their ignoble and miserable death, but themselves. Their characters prove to be their fate. We now find ourselves not in the farms of Sienese country, but in the city of Siena itself, almost always in a somber, depressing bookshop that has become a sort of trap from which there is no escape. For some time prior to the opening of the book, the protagonists have been leading a life riddled with debts, cheating, and supreme indifference. Much like other Tozzian heroes, Giulio, Niccolò, and Enrico Gambi seem to be bent upon destroying the little shop they have inherited from their father, and, by so doing, wipe out the last vestige of his memory.

Their incredibly poor management and business practice have forced them to borrow money from a kind friend, the Cavaliere Orazio Nicchioni, who has signed a promissory note for them. For several months, they have forged his signature on additional notes, promptly cashed by the bank, and their debt has now mounted to fifty thousand liras, a sum of money they can conceivably repay only at the cost of extraordinary sacrifices. Yet, while on the one hand they appear to be indifferent to their disastrous financial affairs, squandering their money on refined and expensive fruits and meats, they also dread the coming of the day of reckoning—the moment when they shall be forced to give a public account of their fraudulent scheme. The greater part of the book is given over to creating the special atmosphere in which the three brothers live, their fears, and their gluttonous pleasures. Visitors to the bookshop are few and customers even fewer. The sporadic visits of their friends have the functional role of allowing the personality of the three brothers to become more sharply delineated. The insularity of their lives, their unwillingness to confront realistically their irresponsible fiscal situation, becomes more clearly understandable in the light of their incredible vanity and egocentricity. The voice of their conscience turns out to be a faithful friend, Nisard, a student of art, a scholarly bibliophile and historian: it is he who makes them realize the opportunities they have missed to lead a meaningful and productive existence.

The drama of the Gambi brothers explodes suddenly one

day when, quite accidentally, their fraudulent scheme is un-covered by one of the bank's tellers. The three brothers find themselves with the prospect of a trial they cannot possibly win and the inevitable loss of their reputation that will write them off, once and for all, from their community. The possibility of being found guilty proves to be too hard to bear for Giulio, who commits suicide by hanging himself in the dark bookshop. His brother Niccolò sets himself to re-store a minimum of integrity to his name so that he might earn a livelihood without leaving his native city. He is helped by a favorable judgment of the court that has found him and Enrico innocent of the charge of fraud. With the assistance of his wife and of a few generous friends, he begins a new life as an insurance agent. But his dishonest past weighs heavily on his conscience, all the more since he and Enrico have placed the entire blame for their fraud on their dead brother. Niccolò begins suffering first from insomnia then from deliriums and, after a brief illness, dies of rheumatic apoplexy.

A similarly unhappy fate awaits the last surviving mem-ber of the unhappy trio, Enrico. After the death of his two brothers, Enrico rapidly sinks into a degrading kind of life, drinking and begging, spending his nights in public parks, in the streets, or wherever else he happens to find himself. He is finally taken to a local sanitarium where a short time later he dies of a blood infection caused by a serious case of gout which has afflicted him for some years.

As with his earlier works, *Tre croci* is less a novel of plot than one of characters masterfully and soberly created by Tozzi: the three brothers, with all their idiosyncracies, their human flaws, are portrait studies of unusual depth. Their gluttonous feasts, their eruptions of rage, their irresponsible behavior hardly conceal and much less alleviate their un-conscious fear, a kind of subterranean dread that their exist-ence will no longer provide them with pleasures they enjoy at a heavy price. They are doomed to wait, with all the anxiety and trepidation of a human being expecting his final confrontation with truth, for the ruin and shame they know they justly deserve. They exist only to allow their inevitable tragedy to take place and run its course, and their expectation is subtly deepened by the somber descriptions of Siena, their prison. In the words of Giorgio Luti, "Siena itself, which is the only background of the novel, lives of its own autonomous life, first among [its] personages." Siena is, indeed, the hostile and inclement city "Tozzi knew in the years of his 'pathological' youth." Its inhabitants are the characters peopling the novel, "absurd personages of a ghostlike humanity," prisoners of a human condition one can escape only at the end of one's life. The gloomy stillness of the city, its dark, labyrinthine, narrow streets weigh heavily upon the action of the book. By contrast, the vibrant sunsets and the descriptions of the lovely countryside surrounding Siena serve as apt contrasts to the predicament of the three brothers, whose existence has become as twisted as the streets of their city. The setting becomes an integral part of the narrative, a kind of musical background to a symphony of despair and desolation.

"Niccolò: wake up!" shouts Giulio at the opening of the novel. His cry is a plea replete with anticipatory signals whose full significance will not be understood until the story has had the chance to unfold, gaining its momentum despite the slow, deliberately monotonous pace of the novel. Here as well as elsewhere in Tozzi's fiction, to wake up means to open our eyes to a dreadful reality in which we find ourselves, the reality of a life made squalid and hopeless not merely by its incongruity, but by a painfully obvious lack of love and companionship. Without them, life becomes but a series of meaningless and purposeless grotesque acts: the hours spent sleeping when there is work to do; the idle talk about a good table; the nonaction of the three brothers, content to pursue the easy and yet fatal path that can only lead to disaster; the constant bickering and arguing that goes on between them, are yet other reflections of the uneasiness of their own lives.

Invariably in a narrative where the action, or the plot, plays a lesser role, as in the case of *Three Crosses*, the writer works through different structures to achieve the desired effects. The drama of the protagonists unfolds not through descriptions, which could easily have damaged the impartiality of the narration, but through the heated, often depressing and bizarre conversations they have with each other and with their few friends. Tozzi's language is scabrous, excited—with all its curses, its dire predictions of impending disasters, its numerous outbursts of anger and boredom—and as such it effectively reflects the neuroses of the book's central personages. Even their common illness, the gout, becomes symbolic of the sickness that pervades and eventually infects not only their blood but their very souls. Unlike their predecessors, the characters of *Three Crosses* are not humiliated and insulted, nor much less are they victims of an enigmatic destiny. They know beforehand and almost wait anxiously for the disaster that will conclude their preposterous schemings. The promissory note, the famous *cambiale* that is at the center of ever so many feverish conversations and reflections that animate the book, is turned into a tangible sign of the evil that just *is* in their lives, the reminder of a shame that is upon them, a sin they must expiate. It may also be, as Debenedetti persuasively sustains in his essay, "an indirect aggression against their father's memory."

Of the three protagonists, Giulio, presented as "the most melancholy of the Gambi brothers, but also the strongest," remains to the end the most acutely aware of what they have become. He is also, however, the most tragic figure because of his failing to harness whatever strength there was in him to bring about a change to their situation. Indeed, since he engineered the fraudulent scheme of forging the Cavaliere's signature, Giulio must live more intensely than his two brothers in the drama of the dishonesty of which they are guilty and the loneliness to which they are condemned. He has lived, as he acknowledges in a moment of extreme lucidity, "a kind of regularity that seemed to me to be just and appropriate. Now I realize," he continues, "how I have been living only provisionally, until one day some decisive event, such as that of the promissory note, should come along, transforming into weakness whatever had formerly seemed strong and well chosen." His freedom, as he sees it, is in his choice to live or coexist with his fears in a silence that allows him to suffer for himself and for others as well. His loneliness is his meager achievement, the only one his pride can yield. But pride is also what causes him to assume an arrogant, immoral stance that only hastens the end of his miserable existence. "Debts and [promissory] notes," as Giorgio Luti underscores, "are symbols of a provincial society that grants no freedom to the individual, no possible choice, leaving no room to the dream in the increasingly more restless relation between past and present."

It befalls on Giulio, the real protagonist of the tragedy of the Gambi brothers, to articulate through his reflections shortly before he commits suicide, the nature of their predicament, the very reason why life can no longer be understood neither as a challenge, nor as a source of pleasure:

> He felt that the act of living had become for him a totally involuntary matter. He no longer cared about anything, and the voices of the others speaking in the next room seemed as though checked by some obstacle, which prevented them from reaching him or including him in their circle. . . . He could not even be sad or worried; an unchanging and fatal clarity in a medley of recollections and thoughts reminded him that he could do nothing to change the state of affairs. He felt that all around him was crumbling and he could find no solid basis in which to take a decision. He even felt that it would always be impossible for him to account for this conscious silence and emptiness that overwhelmed him.

Passages such as the one just quoted give us at least a feeling of the modernity and relevance of a writer whose work, seemingly written in the conventions of *verismo*, could easily be mistaken for regionalistic. A more careful analysis of the book quickly dispels such a notion. True enough, judging at least from his settings, Tozzi was indeed a provincial. But the real reason for his insistence upon locating most of his fiction in Siena had less to do with prevailing fashions at that time (one thinks here of Fogazzaro,

Deledda, Pirandello, d'Annunzio, and a score of other contemporaries of his) than with his determination to write
from his own experience. He was less interested in giving
us yet another believable tableau of life in the provinces—
although judging from his work he eminently did succeed in
this—than in creating a world riddled by violence and
haunted by dark fears. He accepted the gamble of being
classified as just another regionalistic writer in an era when
Italian culture was striving to shed its provincialism and
insularity and insert itself in the mainstream of European
letters, by creating characters and landscapes that were
nothing if not universal symbols of the suffering and estrangement of the whole of mankind. Thus, for all the
deceptive realism of his fiction, Tozzi was hardly interested
in reality as such. Depicting life on the farms, or in a small
bookshop in the silent, sleepy, and yet terrifying city of
Siena, was for him but a way to descend into the mysterious
regions of private consciousness and explore its fragility.
"Our sweetest and tenderest feelings must go through a
fatal necessity which completely disregards them. In Pirandello there is laughter, but never joyfulness. . . . next to
goodness, there is always the threat of evil and meanness,"
so Tozzi wrote about one of the writers he held in great
esteem. Pirandello's "human world is conceived as a kind of
punishment, which often forces it to become twisted and
limited." These accurate insights apply as much to Tozzi
as they were meant to apply to Pirandello.

While to some extent the problem of good and evil is
most central in his stories, it is the manner in which it is
worked out in the world of the human heart, rather than in
the world of action, that matters. And that world, as Tozzi
rightly perceives, never yields easy answers to troublesome
and complex problems. Unlike the masters of *verismo*
whose work he admired, he did not attribute the defeat and
eventual destruction to which his characters are inexorably
doomed to economic, and much less, to religious causes.
Unlike the naturalists, he did not believe in and was therefore incapable of dramatizing the connection between cause
and effect. Instead, he contented himself with painting the

fragmentation of human life whose pieces, like those of a shattered mirror, "can't be fitted together," as Ben Johnson notes.

In the area of language Tozzi left his unmistakable mark on contemporary Italian literature. "It is not so much his personality as a man, and its reflection on his works," continues Johnson, "that has counted with writers who have come after him, as the influence he has had upon the Italian written language. Every great writer rapes the language he is given to use, bending it to his own end, and Tozzi did just that. . . . in the last couple of years of his life he expunged from his writings all verbiage, stripped it to its essentials, to the neglect even of grammar and syntax and to the horror of purists." In a manner not at all dissimilar from Verga's and Svevo's, Tozzi set for himself the task to create—there is no better term for it—a language through which he could give life to the sordid, sensual, and violent collection of Sienese peasants and small merchants that people his world. Through what eventually became his style, he succeeded in conjuring up the stifling, alienated vision that emerges bit by bit from the haunted novels of a haunted man. Confronted by an existence deprived of all traditional logic, Tozzi's characters must sit, like Beckett's heroes, waiting not for Godot, but for a death that will free them from their anxieties and dread. "The new novel, discovered and at once realized by Tozzi," concludes Debenedetti in his essay, "looks at psychology from a nocturnal side, in a zone that affords no mundane explanations, does not conceive of problems that may be explained with a ruler and a compass, a zone that is more precisely called the psyche." Unlike Svevo, whose major novel *The Confessions of Zeno* was to appear barely three years after the death of the Sienese, Tozzi never found in irony or humour the element that would enable him to resolve the tensions of his tales. Gloomy, somber almost to excess, the characters of Tozzi's world live out the consequences of an alienated existence, and in this sense they have at least something in common with the creations of Luigi Pirandello. As we have seen, however, Pirandello's characters come forward to the center of the stage to argue out their case, and attempt to resolve their predicament by a deceit that becomes a kind of *modus vivendi*, an arrangement that will permit them to make peace with their situation. Not so in Tozzi's case: his characters are destined to live an existence that both psychologically and physically constitutes a rejection of an unhealthy family bond. "We have," writes Debenedetti, "a stage crowded with flesh-and-blood presences of reincarnated memories, which push their way, confusedly, to the foreground, without any rationale of time, space, or causality, bound together only by their power of vexation and evil." It ultimately matters little, in the context of the attitude of Tozzi's characters, whether society expects them to be proficient students, successful farmers and overseers, or astute businessmen. Inevitably they are asked to accept a legacy of mores and values they find, in the depth, to be thoroughly repulsive.

Everywhere, in the private life as well as in the artistic world of Federigo Tozzi, there are tangible signs of an estrangement that has chocked off the possibility of happiness as well as the impelling need of human companionship and communion. Lonely, alienated, wretched, the heroes of Tozzi truly live, *ante litteram*, the ordeal of contemporary man, looking everywhere for answers to the riddle of existence. Their drama is ours: and our responsiveness to it is what ultimately cancels the chronological distance that separates us from him.

Selected Bibliography

General Works on Italian Literature

Apollonio, Mario. *I Contemporanei*. New rev. ed. Milan: La Scuola, 1970.

Babou, V. *Civilisation italienne*. Paris: Didier, 1965.

Barié, Ottavio. *L'Italia nell'Ottocento*. Turin: UTET, 1964.

Binni, Walter. *La Poetica del decadentismo italiano*. 1936. Reprint, rev. Florence: Sansoni, 1969.

Bo, Carlo. *L'eredità di Leopardi e altri saggi*. Florence: Vallecchi, 1964.

Borlenghi, Aldo. *Narratori dell'Ottocento e del primo Novecento*. 5 vols. Milan: Ricciardi, 1961–66.

Capuana, Luigi. *Studi sulla letteratura italiana contemporanea*. 1st series, Milan: Brigola, 1880; 2nd series, Catania: Giannotta, 1882.

————. *Gli "ismi" contemporanei*. Catania: Giannotta, 1898.

Cecchi, Emilio and Sapegno, Natalino, eds. *Storia della letteratura italiana*, vols. 8 and 9. Milan: Garzanti, 1968–69.

Croce, Benedetto. *La letteratura della nuova Italia*. 6 vols. Bari: Laterza, 1946–51.

David, Michel. *La psicanalisi nella cultura italiana*. Milan: Boringhieri, 1966.

Debenedetti, Giacomo. *Il romanzo del Novecento*. Milan: Garzanti, 1971.

De Castris, A. Leone. *La polemica sul romanzo storico*. Bari: Cressati, 1959.

De Robertis, Giuseppe. *Scrittori del Novecento*. Florence: Le Monnier, 1940.

————. *Altro Novecento*. Florence: Le Monnier, 1962.

Garin, Eugeno. *Cronache di filosofia italiana* (1900–1943). Bari: Laterza, 1958.

———. *La Cultura italiana tra '800 e '900*. Bari: Laterza, 1962.

Guarnieri, Silvio. *Cinquant'anni di narrativa in Italia*. Florence: Parenti, 1955.

Marzot, Giulio. *Battaglie veristiche dell'Ottocento*. Milan: Principato, 1941.

Pacifici, Sergio, ed. *From Verismo to Experimentalism: Essays on the Modern Italian Novel*. Bloomington, Indiana: Indiana University Press, 1969.

Pancrazi, Pietro. *Ragguagli di Parnaso*. 3 vols. Milan: Ricciardi, 1967.

Personé, Luigi. *Scrittori italiani moderni e contemporanei*. Florence: Olschki, 1968.

Petrocchi, Giorgio. *Il romanzo storico italiano nell'800*. Turin: Eri, 1967.

Phelps, Ruth Shepard. *Italian Silhouettes*. 1924. Reprint. Freeport, N.Y.: Books for Libraries Press, 1968.

Pomilio, Mario. *Dal naturalismo al verismo*. Napoli: Liguori, 1966.

Russo, Luigi. *I Narratori: 1850–1957*. Milan: Principato, 1958.

Salinari, Carlo. *Miti e coscienza del decadentismo italiano*. Milan: Feltrinelli, 1960.

Serra, Renato. *Scritti*. Edited by Giuseppe De Robertis and A. Grilli. Florence: Le Monnier, 1958.

Tonelli, Luigi. *Alla ricerca della personalità*. Catania: Studio Editoriale moderno, 1929.

Varese, Claudio. *Cultura letteraria contemporanea*. Pisa: Listri-Nischi, 1951.

Vené, Gianfranco. *Letteratura e capitalismo in Italia dal '700 ad oggi*. Milan: Sugar, 1963.

Vittorini, Domenico. *High Points in the History of Italian Literature*. New York: David McKay, 1958.

———. *The Modern Italian Novel*. 1930. Reprint. New York: Russell & Russell, 1967.

West, Paul. *The Modern Novel*. Vol. 2. New York: Hillary House, 1963.

Selected References

The following is a highly selective listing of essays and books which I found to be particularly helpful and stimulating in the course of writing this book. Whenever possible, care has been taken to include critical material in English. In some cases, for the sake of convenience, certain titles are listed in a shortened version. Complete information pertaining to such works will be found in the Selected Bibliography. The following abbreviations have been used:

LICr   *Letteratura Italiana: le Correnti*, vol. 2. Milan: Marzorati, 1956
LIC   *Letteratura Italiana: i Contemporanei*, vol. 1. Milan: Marzorati, 1963
LNI   *La Letteratura della nuova Italia*, by Benedetto Croce
LIM   *Letteratura Italiana: i Maggiori*, vol. 2. Milan: Marzorati, 1956
NA   *Nuova antologia*
PMLA   *Publication of Modern Language Association*
RdP   *Ragguagli di Parnaso*, by Pietro Pancrazi
SdLI   *Storia della letteratura italiana*, ed. by Emilio Cecchi and Natalino Sapegno

Additional works on Italian literature, particularly those dealing primarily with the background of the modern Italian novel and the early part of the nineteenth century may be found in *The Modern Italian Novel from Manzoni to Svevo*, pp. 184–86 in this series.

BACKGROUND OF THE MODERN ITALIAN NOVEL

There is ample material available to the reader interested in extending his knowledge of the period under consideration. Among the best treatments of the history of modern Italy are Denis Mack Smith's masterful *Italy: A Modern History* (Ann Arbor: University of Michigan, 1959) and Salvatore Saladino's *Italy from Unification to 1919* (N.Y.: Thomas Y. Crowell, 1970). Massimo Salvadori's *Italy* (Englewood Cliffs, N.J.: Prentice Hall, 1965) is a limpid summary of the history of Italy. On the cultural side, there is much merit in the essays by Mario Apollonio, in his *I Contemporanei*, particularly the chapter "Crisi d'anteguerra." The long chapter by Norberto Bobbio, "Profilo ideologico del Novecento," in Cecchi and Sapegno, *SdLI*, 3:121–28, is very rewarding for its philosophical insights. Silvio Guarnieri's fine study, *Cinquant'anni di narrativa in Italia* is particularly stimulating. Other important essays include Sergio Antonielli's "Dal Decadentismo al Neorealismo," in *LIC*, 2:897–936, and the long introductory essay by Aldo Borlenghi in his five-volume anthology *Narratori dell'Ottocento*. Among the more general studies of the period see the bulky, absorbing volume by Ottavio Barié, *L'Italia nell'Ottocento* (Turin: UTET, 1964) containing photographs, statistics, and a helpful bibliography. On the question of the historical novel, the following are useful: Giorgio Petrocchi, *Il romanzo storico nell'Ottocento italiano* (Turin: RAI, 1967); Guido Baldi, *Giuseppe Rovani e il problema del romanzo storico* (Florence: Olschki, 1967) and A. Leone De Castris, *La polemica sul romanzo storico* (Bari: Cressati, 1959). Two shorter, but clear treatments of the problems of the novel and *la questione della lingua* are Kalikst Morawski's *Il romanzo storico italiano nell'epoca del Risorgimento* (Wroclaw, Ossolineum, 1970) and T. Gwynfor Griffith, *Italian Writers and the "Italian" Language* (Hull, Yorkshire: University of Hull, 1967).

The essay by Mario Pomilio, "L'eclissi del Verismo," in *Il ponte* 24, 2 (1968), 228–42, brings into perspective the polemics on the problem of the novel in Italy at the end of the last century. The role of the literary magazines (and of *La Voce* in particular) in Italian cultural life of our century may be grasped by reading Carlo Martini's study *"La Voce," Storia e bibliografia* (Pisa: Nistri-Lischi, 1956); the edition of the most important pieces that were published in *La Voce* have been collected by Angelo Romanò, *La cultura italiana del '900 attraverso le riviste: "La Voce,"* vol. 3 (Turin: Einaudi, 1960). The pages by Giuseppe Petronio in his *L'attività letteraria in Italia* (Palermo: Palumbo, 1966) succeed in giving us an insight into the literary convolutions of Italy from the Middle Ages to our own time. Giulio Cattaneo's essay, "Prosatori e critici dalla Scapigliatura al verismo," (in *SdLI*, vol. 8, pp. 269–488), is immensely rewarding.

LUIGI CAPUANA

In recent years there has been a notable renaissance of interest in Capuana's work as a critic and as a novelist. In English the reader may find two monographs particularly helpful: Eugene Scalia, *Luigi Capuana and His Times* (N.Y.: S. F. Vanni, 1952) and Vincenzo Paolo Traversa, *Luigi Capuana Critic and Novelist* (The Hague: Mouton, 1968). The role played by Capuana in the closing decades of the last century is reviewed by Mario Pomilio in his study *Dal Naturalismo al Verismo*, pp. 121–56. Hilda L. Norman wrote a carefully documented analysis of the use Capuana made of science and witchcraft in his novels, "The Scientific and Pseudo-Scientific in the Works of L. C.," *PMLA* 53 (1938), 869–85, while E. A. Walker addressed himself to Capuana's technique in his article "Structural Techniques in L. C.'s Novels," *Italica* 42 (1965), 266–75. For an examination of Capuana's role as a critic, the reader may turn to Achille Pelizzari's *Il pensiero e l'arte di L. C.* (Naples: F. Perella, 1919); Gaetano Trombatore, "L. C. critico," *Belfagor* 4 (1949), 410–24; P. Mazzamuto, "L. C. critico," in *Tra filologi e critici* (Palermo: Palumbo, 1968), pp. 99–140.

Capuana's critical pronouncements quoted in chapter 2 may be found in *Cronache letterarie* (Catania: Giannotta, 1899); *Libri e teatro* (Catania: Giannotta, 1892); *Per l'arte* (Catania: Giannotta, 1884); as well as in the two volumes listed in the "General Works on Italian Literature" in this bibliography. Corrado Di Blasi's *L.C. Vita, amicizia, relazioni letterarie* (Mineo: Biblioteca Capuana, 1954) is an authoritative biographical account of Capuana. His modernity and worth as a critic is examined by Giorgio Luti in "Capuana moderno." *Inventario* 6 (May–Dec. 1954), 146–54. Ettore Caccia's essay on Capuana in *LIC*, pp. 2896–927, is a useful survey, as is the older piece by Luigi Tonelli, *Alla ricerca della personalità*, pp. 3–28. Croce's chapter in *LNI*, 3:103–20, is still quite instructive.

GABRIELE D'ANNUNZIO

So large, varied, and controversial is the critical bibliography on d'Annunzio that it is almost embarrassing to select a few of the best and most representative works on him. From the biographical point of view, we may begin, in English, with Frances Winwar's *Wingless Victory. A Dual Biography of Gabriele d'Annunzio and Eleonora Duse* (New York: Harper & Row, 1956) and in Italian, with Tommaso Antongini's *Vita segreta di Gabriele d'Annunzio*, (Milan: Mondadori, 1938). Among the earliest estimates of d'Annunzio, the classic items are Francesco Flora's *D'A.* (1926; reprint ed., Messina: Principato, 1935); Giuseppe A. Borgese's *G. d'A.* (1909; reprint ed., Milan: Mondadori, 1951); A. Rhode's *D'Annunzio: the Poet as Superman* (London: Weidenfeld & Nicolson, 1958); and

Alfredo Gargiulo's ground-breaking work, *G. d'A.* (1912; reprint ed., rev., Milan: Mondadori, 1958). The large volume by Eurialo De Michelis, *Tutto d'Annunzio* (Milan: Feltrinelli, 1960) is particularly useful for the summaries and critical insights it offers on every single work of its subject. Giuseppe Petronio's survey in *LIM*, 2:1305–30, is a lean and accurate presentation of the unquestionable flaws and merits of d'A.'s work. More recently, a number of critics have begun reassessing d'A. in the light of different approaches to his work: among such criticism, I found Marziano Guglielminetti's volume *Struttura e sintassi* ("L'orazione del d'A.," pp. 9–63) penetrating; Mario Praz's *La carne, la morte e il diavolo nella letteratura romantica* (*Florence: Sansoni*, 1948) excellent; and his introductory essay to the omnibus volume of d'Annunzio's work, *Poesie, teatro, prose*, ed. Mario Praz and Ferdinando Guerra (Milan: Ricciardi, 1966), pp. vii–xxiv indispensable. The volume contains also a section by Ferdinando Guerra, "Vita e opere," as well as a selected bibliography (pp. xxv–xxxvi and xil–xlvii respectively). The links between d'Annunzio and fascism have been thoroughly analyzed by, among others, Carlo Salinari, *Miti e coscienza*, pp. 29–105, and Giuseppe A. Borgese, *Golia. Marcia del fascismo* (Milan: Mondadori, 1949). Ezio Raimondi's monographic study on d'A. (*SdLI*, 9:3–84) is exhaustive and includes an excellent bibliography of criticism on his subject. Since every major critic has dealt with one or more sides of d'A.'s life, poetics, and literary production, the reader should consult the works of Croce, De Robertis, Gargiulo, Debenedetti, Russo, et al. listed in the "General Works on Italian Literature" in this bibliography.

ANNA NEERA

Thanks to Benedetto Croce's warm appraisal of Neera in his *LNI* (3:121–40), the novelist has fared somewhat better than many of her contemporaries. Aldo Borlenghi's introduction in his fourth volume of *Narratori dell'Ottocento*, pp. 227–36, is lucid and offers a good bibliography. P. Romagnoli Robuschi's "Una scrittrice dimenticata," in *Vita e pensiero* 40 (1957), 437–42, is a sympathetic treatment of his subject. Other items include: Guido Piovene, "Idee e personaggi di Neera," in *Corriere della sera*, May 23, 1943; Giuseppe Ravegnani's *I contemporanei* (Turin: Bocca, 1930), pp. 55–66; Ruth Shepard Phelps, *Italian Silhouettes*, pp. 198–212.

SIBILLA ALERAMO

From the autobiographical point of view, the reader seeking some insights into Aleramo's character should read *Dal mio diario* (Rome: Tumminelli, 1958) and "Esperienze d'una scrittrice," originally delivered as a talk to factory workers in Turin and now available in the Communist review *Rinascita*, May 1952, pp. 293–98. For further biographical details see the interview published by Leone Piccioni in his volume *Confessioni di scrittori* (*Interviste con se stessi*), (Turin: Rai, 1951).

Among the critical essays on Aleramo, the most informative and valuable are: Artal Marzotti, "S. A.," in *LIC*, 1:211–32. The chapter on A. in Luigi Tonelli's *Alla ricerca della personalità*, pp. 143–170, is still valid; Giuseppe Ravegnani's "La Vivanti, l'A. e la letteratura femminile," in *I contemporanei* (Turin: Bocca, 1930), pp. 55–56, reflects what used to be the typical Italian critic's point of view on women intellectuals. Among the fine tributes to Aleramo, published after her death, are Eugenio Montale's "La forza e il segreto di S. A.," in *Corriere della sera*, Jan. 14, 1960, and Enrico Falqui's "S. A. in morte," now reprinted in *Il Novecento letterario* (Florence: Vallecchi, 1961), 3:383–86, which focuses on Aleramo's poetry rather than her fiction.

ALFREDO PANZINI

The popularity of Panzini, at least with the literate segment in Italy, has attracted a great deal of critical material on his life and work. The most recent and most balanced of such monographs is Giorgio De Rienzo's *Alfredo Panzini* (Milan: Mursia, 1968), a thorough examination of the subject's vast literary output. The work carries also a useful, carefully compiled chronological list of Panzini's publications, right down to the individual short stories and essays. Aside from the reviews of varying interest by Gargiulo, De Robertis, Falqui, et al., one may consult Benedetto Croce's essay on P. in *LNI*, 6:338–52. Renato Serra's sympathetic evaluation may be read in *Scritti*, ed. G. De Robertis, pp. 101–47. Carlo Bo's essay "A. P." in *L'eredità di Leopardi e altri saggi*, pp. 145–64, is sensitive, while Antonio Piromalli's piece "Costume e arte in A. P.," *Studi sul Novecento* (Florence: Olschki, 1969), pp. 96–129, is thought-provoking and devastating. Among other monographs, there is also Gabriele Baldini's *A. P.* (Brescia: Morcelliana, 1942). In English, the reader may turn to Vittorini's *The Modern Italian Novel*, pp. 126–37, and Ruth Shepard Phelps's *Italian Silhouettes*, pp. 181–97. The general essay on P. by Arnaldo Bocelli in *LIC*, 1:27–46, is useful. Of particular interest in terms of Panzini's cultural background and development is Claudio Varese's essay "Formazione e Svolgimento di A. P." in *Cultura letteraria contemporanea*, pp. 85–132. The essay by Claudio Marabini, "Nel centenario della nascita: Panzini," in *NA* 489 (1963), 335–52, is a good summing up of Panzini's work and achievement. See also Aldo Borlenghi's *Narratori dell'Ottocento e del primo Novecento*, 5:719–37.

GIUSEPPE A. BORGESE

Borgese the novelist has consistently been slighted in favor of Borgese the critic or the voice of the self-exiled Italian intellectual. There are fleeting references to Borgese in the works by Russo, Cecchi, De Robertis, Gargiulo, Sapegno, et al. (cf. "General Works on Italian Literature," this bibliography). Pancrazi has written a few good pages on Borgese in his *RdP*, "Romanzo di B.," pp. 151–55 and "Tempesta nel nulla," pp. 243–48. The essay by G. A. Peritore in *LIC*, 1:449–68, is a good introduction to Borgese. Gérard Genot is the author of an interesting slim volume, *La première guerre mondiale et le roman: l'Italie. Rubé de Borgese* (Paris: Archives des Lettres Modernes, 4, No. 86, 1968), in which he stresses the connections between the political crises of Italy in the 1910s and her literature, as reflected in B.'s fiction. In English, the chapter by Domenico Vittorini in his book *The Modern Italian Novel*, pp. 225–233, is still a good introduction. Sarah d'Alberti has recently published a monograph, *G. A. B.* (Palermo: Flaccovio, 1971) that takes into account the entire literary activity of her subject.

GRAZIA DELEDDA

The standard critical works on Deledda are Euralio De Michelis's *Grazia Deledda e il Decadentismo* (Florence: La Nuova Italia, 1938), a study of the Sardinian novelist against the background of the literary currents of her time, and the sound volume by Licia Roncarti, *L'arte di G. D.* (Florence: D'Anna, 1949). The most recent study is *G. D.* by Giancarlo Buzzi (Milan: Bocca, 1952). The piece by Domenico Vittorini, "Grazia Deledda and her Early Literary Contacts," in *High Points in the History of Italian Literature* (N.Y.: David McKay, 1958), pp. 249–53, is informative. For a sound short appraisal of the novelist one may read Bonaventura Tecchi, "Quello che è vivo nell'arte di G. D.," in *NA* 95 (1960), 69–84. Pietro Pancrazi's perceptive reviews are still reasonably helpful, and may be read in *RdP*, 2:80–86 and 428–33. See also Borgese, Russo, Tozzi, and Cecchi, listed in the "General Works on Italian Literature," this bibliography. Luigi M. Personé's chapter on Deledda in *Scrittori italiani*, pp. 91–102 is valuable, as is the survey of Giuseppe Petronio in *LIC* 1:137–58. Allen McCormick has written a sympathetic evaluation of *La Madre*, the work he deems Deledda's best: "Grazia Deledda's *La Madre* and the Problem of Tragedy," *Symposium* 22 (1968), 61–71.

MARINO MORETTI

Much has been written about Moretti, as can be ascertained by the impressive bibliography compiled by Francesco Casnati for his volume *M. M.* (Milan: Istituto di Propaganda Libraria, 1952), recently revised and brought up to date for inclusion in the essay included in the volume *LIC*, pp. 649–67. Among the many perceptive articles on Moretti, the following commend themselves for their critical acumen: Luigi Russo, in *I Narratori*, pp. 215–17; Giovanni Titta Rosa, "M. M.," in *Belfagor* 11, No. 5 (1956), 542–56; Emilio Cecchi, "M. M.," in *SdLI* 9:558–91; and the monograph by F. Cazzamini-Mussi, *M. M.* (Florence: Vallecchi, 1931). Borgese's pages in *La vita e il libro* (Bologna: Zanichelli, 1928), pp. 120–28, offer the first sensitive study of Moretti's poetry, while his fiction is considered in *Tempo di edificare* (Milan: Treves, 1924). A readable survey of Moretti's early work may be read in Pietro Pancrazi's "M. M. in verso e in prosa," in *RdP*, pp. 142–52.

LUIGI PIRANDELLO

As with most great literary figures, the bibliography on Pirandello is both vast and impressive. The best and most complete biographical study is Gaspare Giudice's *Luigi Pirandello* (Turin: UTET, 1963) which clearly supersedes Federico Vittore Nardelli's *L'uomo segreto: vita e croci di L. P.* (Milan: Mondadori, 1944). In English, two short but acute studies recommend themselves: Oscar Budel's *Pirandello* (N.Y.: Hillary House, 1966), and Olga Ragusa's well-written *Pirandello* (N.Y.: Columbia Univ. Press, 1968). The essays collected by Glauco Cambon in *Pirandello* (Englewood Cliffs, N.J.: Prentice Hall, 1967) concentrate on producing a picture of its subject's broad interests, and the monograph by Walter Starkie, *L. P.: 1867–1936*, 3rd. ed. rev. (Berkeley: Univ. of California Press, 1965), is a little on the dull side. Pirandello's limitations as a novelist are discussed, with considerable conviction, by E. Allen McCormick, "Luigi Pirandello: Major Writer, Minor Novelist," in *From Verismo to Experimentalism*, ed. by Sergio Pacifici. The interview conducted by Domenico Vittorini is reprinted in *High Points in the History of Italian Literature* (N.Y.: David McKay, 1958) as "Pirandello as I saw Him," pp. 254–67. Beatrice Corrigan's essay "Pirandello and the Theatre of the Absurd," may be read in the *Cesare Barbieri Courier* 8 (1966), 3–6. The volume, *Luigi Pirandello, Naked Masks* (N.Y.: E. P. Dutton, 1952) contains five plays by the Sicilian, an excellent introduction and two appendices, edited and translated by Eric Bentley.

The essay "Humor," together with other essays and papers, is now in Luigi Pirandello, *Saggi, Poesie e Scritti varii*, ed. Manlio Lo Vecchio Musti (Milan: Mondadori, 1960).

In Italian, the most lucid and thought-provoking assessment of Pirandello is A. Leone De Castris's *Storia di Pirandello* (Bari: Laterza, 1962). Excerpts of this work have appeared in English in the anthology edited by Cambon (above) with the title "The Experimental Novelist," pp. 91–102. Antonio Di Pietro's monograph, *Pirandello* (Milan: Vita e pensiero, 1951) is perceptive, as is A. Janner's *L. P.* (Florence: La Nuova Italia, 1960). Giacomo Debenedetti's *Il romanzo del Novecento* contains numerous insights on Pirandello, particularly on this theory of humor. Benedetto Croce's stinging evaluation of P. may be read in *LNI*, 6:353–71. The dualism Art vs. Form is discussed with much persuasion by Adriano Tilgher, in *Studi sul teatro contemporaneo* (Rome: Libreria di Scienze e lettere, 1928). Excerpts of Tilgher's perceptive interpretation appear in English in Cambon's anthological survey (see above).

Gösta Andersson's *Arte e teoria: Studi sulla poetica del giovane Luigi Pirandello* (Stockholm: Almquist & Wiksell, 1966) and the more recent Claudio Vicentini's *L'estetica di P.* (Milan: Mursia, 1970) are complete examinations of the sources of Pirandello's poetics. Luigi M. Personé's "Pirandello, scrittore umoristico," in *Scrittori italiani*, pp. 57–74, once again stresses the special brand of humor that gives Pirandello's opus its special place in Italian literature. For a convincing treatment of Pirandello's poetics, see also Renato Barilli's *La barriera del Naturalismo* (Milan: Mursia, 1964), pp. 9–30. Pirandello's language is discussed with rare acumen by Piero Raffa in "La crisi del linguaggio naturalista," in his *Avanguardia e realismo* (Milan: Rizzoli, 1967), pp. 9–38, and by Filippo Puglisi, *Pirandello e la sua lingua*, 2nd ed. (Milan: Cappelli, 1968). For a particularly penetrating analysis of Pirandello's original contribution to the art of the novel, see Mariziano Guglielminetti's "Il soliloquio di P.," in *Struttura e sintassi del romanzo italiano* (Rome: Silva, 1964), pp. 64–117.

For a broader analysis of Pirandello's work, the introductory essay by Aldo Borlenghi (in *Narratori dell'Ottocento*, 5:401–26) is both precise and illuminating, as is Giovanni Macchia's chapter on Pirandello, in *SdLI*, 9:440–88.

The complete bibliography of Pirandello's works was compiled by M. Lo Vecchio Musti, *Bibliografia di P.*, 2 vols. (Milan: Mondadori, 1937–40 and 1952). A thorough list of critical material on P. may be found in A. Barbina's *Bibliografia della critica pirandelliana, 1889–1961* (Florence: Le Monnier, 1967).

FEDERIGO TOZZI

Up until a few years ago, the work of Federigo Tozzi was a garden cultivated by relatively few critics. Among the first to write about him were Giuseppe A. Borgese, whose numerous reviews constituting moving and sympathetic assessments of the Sienese novelist may be read in *Tempo di edificare* (Milan: Treves, 1924), pp. 23–67 and 118–27, and Eurialo De Michelis, *Saggio su Tozzi* (Florence: La Nuova Italia, 1936). Ferruccio Ulivi is the author of two monographs on Tozzi, *F. T.* (Brescia: Morcelliana, 1940) and the more recent and complete *F. T.* (Milan: Mursia, 1962). Ulivi is also responsible for the essay on Tozzi in *LIC*, 1:469–91. The last three titles contain also a rather complete, if uncritically prepared bibliography. Guorgio Luti has written on Tozzi in the context of early twentieth-century Italian and European literature, "L'esperienza di F. T.," in *Narrativa italiana dell'Otto-Novecento* (Florence: Sansoni, 1954), pp. 167–215.

The most original and brilliant critic of Tozzi was Giacomo Debenedetti, whose lectures on T. delivered at the University of Rome in the early sixties are now part of the volume *Il romanzo del Novecento*. An English translation of a section of that book is included in Sergio Pacifici's *From Verismo to Experimentalism*, pp. 102–19. Aldo Borlenghi's introductory essay in his *Narratori*, 5:945–71, and the bibliography that follows it, are certainly worth reading.

For the most recent critical work on Tozzi, one must turn to F. N. Cimmino's *Il mondo e l'arte di F. T.* (Rome: Giovanni Volpe Ed., 1966). A special symposium on Tozzi was organized in the spring of 1970, with the participation of outstanding critics and writers (Alberto Moravia, Geno Pampaloni, Luigi Baldacci, among them). The proceedings of that symposium were made available to me in mimeographed form by Geno Pampaloni, editor-in-chief of Vallecchi Publishing Co. It is my understanding that the various lectures and discussions of that symposium will eventually appear in book form.

Index